Chellaston Working Lives

An Oral History - Then and Now

1930 – 2012

Mick and Carol Appleby

Chellaston History Group

Printed by Go Digital Print (Derby) Ltd. 62 - 64 Osmaston Rd. Derby DE1 2HZ

ISBN 978-0-9533410-3-0

Introduction

Following the success of "Chellaston Voices", Chellaston History Group asked us to record more people's memories of Chellaston. It was decided to record memories of people's jobs both yesterday and today. This would not only record the past but also create a living history for the future, of present working lives. Rolls-Royce workers have been included because, as in every part of Derby, Chellaston has so many of them. Wherever possible, we tried to find comparative yesterday's and today's workers for each chosen occupation. However, in the case of the Pharmacy and Post Office we recorded one person to represent both past and present.

The extracts in this book are taken from transcripts of recordings with 14 people, carried out between 2007 and 2012, mainly on a Marantz Professional Digital Recorder bought with a grant from East Midlands Co-op. The transcripts replicate, as faithfully as possible, the phraseology and expressions of the participants

Some words have been added to the text to aid meaning; these are indicated by the use of brackets.

Any additional comments are in bold.

It should be stressed that these memories and comments represent the personal views and opinions of the people recorded.

Whilst recording, it became obvious that many people had fascinating experiences which did not always touch upon Chellaston. We felt that it would be wrong not to include these within the book. The amount of material produced has meant that a second book of recordings will be published to complement this one, towards the end of 2013.

One participant, retired Police Constable, Paul Sharman, died on Jan. 1st 2012 whilst on a cruise near Gran Canaria. He had made a marvellous contribution to the book and it is a very sad loss.

Mick and Carol Appleby

Nov. 2012

Further copies of this book are available from Chellaston History Group:
Email: chellastonhistorygroup@googlemail.com Tel: 013322 701210

Thanks are due to the following people:

The 14 contributors, who freely gave their time, often in long sessions in front of a recorder, and their permission to publish their memories.

East Midlands Co-op, for their magnificent gesture in providing funds to help this project.

Chellaston History Group Committee for their support, suggestions and enthusiasm for the project.

We particularly wish to thank Anne Haywood, Susan Smith, Muriel Jones and Gill Donaldson, who helped with transcribing the recordings. They spent many hours carefully listening to and translating participants' oral responses into accurate word documents. Their attention to detail and sheer hard work is greatly appreciated.

We have done our best to trace owners of photographs and thank everyone who gave permission for their use, including Derby Evening Telegraph (one photograph)). We apologise for any photographs inadvertently used without consent.

Contents

POLICE – THEN

Paul Sharman and Wayne Johnson

Chellaston Police Constables:

Paul from 1969 to late 80s and Wayne approx. 1986 to 1993.

From left: Wayne Johnson, Paul Sharman

Sadly, Paul (above right) died on Jan.1ˢᵗ 2012 after he had contributed to our oral history project, and we pay tribute to his long service in the community.

Background

Paul: I was born in Chesterfield, January 1948. We lived at a bungalow which kept us self-sufficient in produce and hens. My father was born in 1889; (he) was a foreman shunter in Mansfield goods yard for 50 years. My Mum, Muriel Sims, was his second wife. She did a lot of service in her younger years before marrying my father. We lived in a little hamlet with about a dozen houses, if that. We used to go into the fields and play. When my dad retired, we moved to a little shop at Hillstown near Bolsover near Chesterfield. Unfortunately my dad was taken ill and died with acute septicaemia. I think I was 9 then.

I finished my education at Moorfield County Secondary School. I did fancy being a draughtsman but unfortunately didn't do too well with me school exams and so I went into the police cadets.

Wayne: I was born in 1955 in Chesterfield. My dad had been a long-term soldier; he'd been in Malaya in the Malayan uprising and had then gone to work for the National Coal Board driving a big earth moving machine on the pits. Me mother had been a trimmer, which is an upholsterer on vehicles at Reeve Coach Builders at Chesterfield.

I was brought up on the edge of a village called Heath. One side of the village was mines, but the end that I lived was all farms. The nice thing was we'd got a lot of fields and an old railway cutting and woods we used to play in, so any mischief we got up to wasn't seen.

I'd been trained as a trimmer, a vehicle upholsterer, and the fuel crisis hit the airlines we were contracted to, so as the airlines finished, so did this company and I'd got to find another job; and it was either go in the forces, which I quite fancied – me dad had been a soldier – or the police force.

Qualifications and Training

Paul: I suppose in those naïve years you wanted to try and put a few things right and help the public. (Entry was) by 4 or 5 GCEs, (minimum) height 5'10", but being an ex-cadet I was allowed to take an entrance exam. Obviously they liked you fit - that was the main priority.

I went to Pannal Ash, Police College just outside Harrogate. The standard was very high. Where we used to eat was very similar to a public school: all the senior officers used to sit at the head of the table.

In class this teacher was walking up and down explaining this particular offence. The next thing I knew he'd dragged me across to him, and said, "That's the battery, the assault is the threat!" It put me on me metal, shall we say! There was firearms discharged in the classroom – blanks obviously - a 2.2 rifle in this case and one or two of us shot out of their seats!

Swimming baths at college were more or less just dug out in a field with a corrugated tin building round them – in January they were freezing. You'd be down there at 6 in the morning doing the rescue type of stuff before your breakfast.

They also on one occasion stuffed us into a hut very close to the swimming baths to experience a crowd-controlling type of gas. We all piled out after several seconds - tears and coughing! I don't think they do that sort of thing nowadays.

Wayne: I think if you'd got at least three CSEs at the time, you could sit the entrance exam. If you'd got A levels or anything higher, you automatically went forward for your interview, an induction course and assessment day in the gym at Butterley Hall headquarters, then chest x-rays and everything at Matlock hospital.

Then it was your 13 weeks training at Pannal Ash. It was very tough from the minute you got off the coach from Derbyshire. You were drilled and marched and straight back to your dormitory, full of beds and lockers just like the forces and you'd got to do your bed-packs as the army. When the drill sergeant was yelling and screaming at somebody, it would be quite funny because it would be your turn next. Some chaps went back on the coach the same day – they weren't havin' that!

For the first 5 weeks I could have cried at the drop of the hat because the discipline was totally unbelievable; it's like the forces - they bring things out of you that you don't know you've got.

They'd got a complete village, within the grounds – there was housing estates, roads. They would stage a car crash - two cars – bang! – steam everywhere and you've got to go and sort it out. Your class and instructor were watching how you handled it – no different to being on the street because people watch the officer do his bit. It was great!

You did your proper pass-out parade and everything and then it was back to wherever you were posted.

Starting Work.

Paul: You'd got to learn the psychology of the job from scratch in those days. We came out of training school, had a weekend off, then Monday at Ilkeston. They gave you a beat book which contained all the beats of Ilkeston with all the phone boxes - (for) making points every hour - pre-radio days. An experienced officer would show you the routes to take. There was no tutor constable – you were straight out on your own the second night; on nights for a week. That's how it was; if you got into a bit of a mess you needed to talk yourself out of it.

Wayne: My first station was Peartree, Normanton - a very tough place. The police station was a very basic series of Nissen huts - an old Air Raid Precautions station - at the junction of Vulcan St. and Peartree Rd.

You'd get introduced to everybody on your shift, then you'd be taken out for a month with a tutor - constable. They taught you hands on, on the streets, how to talk to people, how to handle people properly and how to work a beat. I'd never dealt with any different races and then all of a sudden there it was, all there for me to learn. But it was good groundin'.

You didn't walk too fast or you would look like Charlie Chaplin going up the road; you took your time observing what was round. You'd probably meet the sergeant at a certain time at the top of the road, when you first join, 'cus you're kept an eye on. I used hand – weights at home so I could make my arms strong, so if I'd got someone I could hang on to them You'd get some people who'd hold their hands out – "I'll come with you." Some, it would take two or three of you to hold them down. A lot of incidents were difficult to handle because (of the) language barrier, but you muscle through.

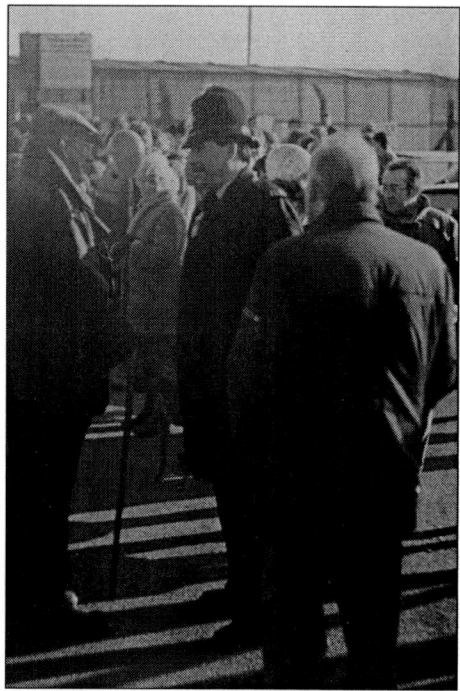

PC Wayne Johnson and panda car

PC Wayne Johnson on duty at Aston Lane proposed travellers' site in the 80s

PC Paul Sharman with his Long Service Award.

Uniform

Paul: We were issued with a woollen one and also a smart Barathea (fine textured cloth) uniform for summer use, made by Smith's of Drewry Lane. On the wrist was like a bandsman's scroll that went up the sleeve. By the time Wayne joined, they'd changed the companies and the quality did go down. The old Smith's uniforms, had an attached belt – held you together better. Then they went on to the separate belts.

I think the later Derbyshire (helmets) were like a cone; the ones with the point on were the Derby Borough (with) a leather inner band – which was quite comfortable. They all used to come off pretty easy if you was shaken about!

Wayne: When I joined, the uniform was thick, woolly, almost like a battle dress. They used to laugh at us in training school - other forces had got nice, fine cloths and Derbyshire would turn up with this woolly uniform that you had the devil to put a crease in. I was given a shirt that you had to button the collars on when I first started (like) my granddad used to have! It soon changed from that to a denim–type shirt. (They) were marvellous - you couldn't wear 'em out.

(Our helmets) used to have a bit of a point on at one stage, and then it went to like a fireman's style, Roman style. They've got fibreglass and stuff in 'em nowadays.

Boots

Wayne: (Boots) were supplied at one time - Technic. Good quality. Leather soles, though – if you're not careful, you'd slip all over the place, especially with Peartree because all the paths up there were usually black builders' brick. There was a bobby down at Full St called Artie Shaw, he'd got cobbling skills and first thing you did, you went down to see him; you'd have a commando sole put on your leather boots, then they'd last twice as long.

Paul: Two pairs a year, I believe, the issue was.

Equipment – truncheons, handcuffs and torch

Paul: You had the old fashioned handcuffs, like a shackle with a separate key, whereas now they have the automatic latch-on types that snap on. At Ilkeston on nights, you used to have to present all your accoutrements on parade. I got a right rollicking one night – the inspector looked down me keyhole in me handcuffs and seen a bit o' fluff. Military discipline! Nothing wrong with it – we used to have a laugh about it after.

As the years went on it became the norm to handcuff most people, whether they were violent or otherwise; in the early days we probably wouldn't have used 'em, with co-operative prisoners.

(The truncheons were) about 14 inch. (You needed them) in our day, because you was more alone, even in the night time. They used to teach you pulling it out of the pocket with your thumb, swinging it around, (to) land in the palm of your hand. You was always taught to avoid the head, unless it was life-threatening. I never used mine in anger, in all honesty, during my whole service.

Wayne: I was issued with the wind-up key handcuffs, like solid iron things, and then it went to the chrome ratchet ones. They were a good bit o' kit, but you'd literally got to wind the things up and when you were struggling wi' somebody they were very heavy. They used to rip your pockets. At Peartree (I used them) about every other day.

(Using truncheons) was down to you. If somebody started playing their fists about, you needed to protect yourself. The radios were not very good. If you caught their elbows, caught them at the back of the wrist, you could render that fist useless; somebody's trying to kick you, you could crack 'em across the knee cap, and they got the message. If you used it right, you really could restrain somebody with it, without having to hit 'em with it – arm locks, things like that.

If you had to break windows to get in at somebody that's collapsed, again your staff, it was always there. If you came across an animal like a cat that had been run over in terrible pain, you'd just have to literally just put it out of its pain.

Chellaston Posting

Paul: I was issued the beat in the late 60s - pre-radio, pre-panda (car) days. We were all walking then. When I first started, the Flatts were there; there was only a few council houses on Maple Drive; Parkway wasn't there either; next to the Red Lion there was a farm – Pedlar Farm. I think the gateway was where the walk- through is now and his farm buildings used to back onto the houses in Station Rd. In the early days we used to have to come out from (St.) Mary's Gate. There were no sub-stations like they'd got later in the years, so we generally got a lift out by one of the outlying patrol cars to start your beat, and latterly we had the panda cars.

In those days the Borough Force finished at the junction of Boulton Lane and Merrill Way. The County used to patrol this side and up to here (Swarkestone Rd). If anything happened en route from St Mary's Gate police station out to Chellaston, you would call the Derby Borough force to deal with it. Obviously you couldn't abandon it, but you'd keep the people pacified or do what you could until the Borough man came and took it from you and then you'd start your normal patrol.

As the panda cars came in, in the early 70s, they doubled the Alvaston beat up, covering the Boulton Lane side of Alvaston and Chellaston as well (because of) lack of man-power.

Wayne: (After) I'd served time at tough areas, Pear Tree, Allenton and Alvaston, I was invited to Chellaston. It was a nice patch, totally different to what I was used to. Decent people you could talk to. Even some of the rum 'uns would talk to you civil, nice.

Chellaston - on the beat

Paul: We used to cycle out from Cotton Lane up to Chellaston. You'd put (your) bottle green Raleigh cycle somewhere you knew was secure and have a walk round or ride down to the Cottage filling station, which was more or less the periphery of your boundary. Joe Hutchinson's, down Thulston Lane, was about the furthest we used to go before we went onto the Rural (patch). (On nights) we only worked 'til about 2 in the mornin'. You'd do your whole shift with your cycle.

View of the Flatts during the 60s from St Peter's Church tower, looking North West towards Derby Rd, prior to building Chellaston Junior School. Foreground: Walker's Farm (now Walker Buildings, High St).

Top of High St. opposite White House Farm. March 1965. This house is now demolished.

Looking up High St. from the junction with Derby Rd. c1980.. Site of old Co-op and Clowes' farm on right.

View from Swarkestone Rd towards The Lawns Hotel c1980

Wayne: Your beat was basically Chellaston itself. You could get drawn off, and frequently did, if there was something happening at Shelton Lock or even Allenton. Occasionally, you would go on the "Rural"; you'd take over the panda patrol car for 4 or 5 days and you'd cover Chellaston, Aston, Weston, Barrow, Thulston and all these areas as Rural Officer. You'd go round the farms, dealing with outlying villages – park the panda car up in the village, say at Aston on Trent where everybody could see it, and then you'd walk. Then another officer would take over for his spell on "Rural" and you'd revert back to your patch.

I'd pick my bike up from the police house on Boulton Lane, cycle into Chellaston. Sometimes you could get out here and they would call you back to Cotton Lane - you'd have to cycle all the way back!

The first thing I did in the area was get to know my shop keepers, so my beat would probably start walking up and down the shops (on Derby Rd) and, "Everybody OK?" Head round the shop doorway –"Are you all right?" Any problems? Usually I got invited for a cup o' tea somewhere down there – little petrol station that's now a Chinese take-away – it was only like a wooden hut - or the garage next to it if there were nobody about.

Then perhaps nip round the corner to Station Rd and into the marquee place, Crockers'. There used to be a couple of farms down at the bottom of Station Rd there, the furthest one was like a market garden at the time and a lot of the stuff in the fields. Sometimes they got pilfering or thieving.

I would go and poke me nose in the pubs. Then I'd usually go up High St. Sometimes I'd pop in the two police houses on St Peter's Rd, nip and see the vicar or somebody at the shops on High St - because a lot of people used to come in Victoria Wine and gossip - if there were anything worth knowing, I'd pick it up. Then, nip in Tom Christie's, the hairdresser's. His mum was very nice and I knew Tom. I'd go up to the farms at the top of the hill. If I'd got any paperwork, things to serve – summonses – I'd get on with that, or any set enquiries.

Typical crimes

Paul: We'd get (lads on motorbikes) on the footpath near the school. Instant justice! Usually a clip round the ear hole. Nobody complained - we knew the parents. We were probably the last era where we did that.

Wayne: A bit of theft, nothing major. You'd get the odd call. One or two people you had to keep your eye on. (On your bike), you were silent. A criminal would be looking round for a panda car to turn up; they certainly were not looking for a bobby on a bike, and if you watched what you were doing, you could be on 'em before they knew where they were. Lads that I'd move on if they were being stupid (would) stand and talk to you, whereas some patches I'd worked, you wouldn't get that – they wouldn't give you time o' day.

If you got any burglaries it was usually someone from out the area. It was mainly anti-social behaviour – youths outside shops, being a bit intimidating. The shopkeepers didn't want it, so they'd phone us and we'd move them on. The butcher's on Derby Rd had some graffiti sprayed on the wall. We caught them and I got the butcher to give us some scrubbing brushes and I made them scrub it off.

Then they decided to build a new estate (Parkway). Our work increased - it was such a big building site. In the middle of the night a kitchen'd disappear - a lot of theft, tools being stolen. We had a problem with big, heavy building lorries. We tried to get the radar team to set up but there was only one. So P.C. and myself got a couple of deck chairs, we got a cardboard box painted black. We sat there (on the main road) with a clipboard and a hairdryer like we were doing speed checks. We'd only been there for half an hour but for the next few days everything went slow through Chellaston - kiddology, but it worked!

Junction of Maple Drive and Derby Rd. Dec. 1975. Peartree Cottage to the right of what is now Parkway

Work in progress on the roundabout at the junction of Maple Drive and Derby Rd

Paperwork

Paul: We got more (then). I had to do my own typing and being a probationer you was told to do your paperwork after your duty time, unpaid – five copies of everything!

Wayne: Just a simple bump (accident) – it'd end up as thick as a telephone directory. Ream after ream of paper!

I was given a key (to the) the Golden Hour Club, on Maple Drive. I could go in there, make myself a cup o' tea, use the toilet and sit and do paperwork - right in the middle of my patch - I could surface at any time I wanted.

New radios

Paul: (They appeared) In the panda days, as I remember. I think the Derby Borough people had got them in the mid to late 60s, but at Mary's Gate we didn't get them until the panda days in about 1970 **(Chellaston was outside the Borough then)**. They used to be terrible. There used to be two pieces to start with, both got a clip on.

Invariably you'd go to a job and you'd put your receiver down somewhere - you normally used to keep 'em in your epaulette - and at the end of the job, you'd leave the premises where you were and leave your radio!

Wayne: The Pye transmitter, little blue things, had got a button on the top for you to press and transmit, and the other one was the receiver, push 'em in your epaulette or probably one in your pocket. When you're dealing with an incident, you've got these two radios – your hands are tied up for a start. When you pressed the transmitter, the little aerial was on a spring and it used to pop up. The trouble is, it either went up your nose, or caught you in the eye!

Paul: The rural car, that always had VHF – a fitted radio. They were pretty good.

Football matches

Paul: You'd have your shift extended without any form o' notice - policing the football match. You might have arranged to do something with the family and you'd end up knocking off about 6 o'clock, instead of your normal 2 o'clock.

Wayne: Your 3 days off came round once a month. If there was a football match on, you could guarantee you would have Saturday cancelled without notice - getting me mac spit all over and pennies thrown at you. You couldn't take your wife or family to Skegness for the day or anything like that, and that really used to annoy me. Later on my sons didn't go in the police force and I think a lot of it was that.

Pit strikes

Paul: The last one - was it '84? - every bit of leave and rest days were cancelled. I don't think I had a day off for almost a year. They were 12 hour shifts, at Swadlincote or Alfreton. One night they had the Kent flying pickets up to the Swadlincote pit, Cadley Hill Colliery. Quite frightening at the time. We were outnumbered for one thing; there was hundreds came this particular evening – a lot of argey - bargey.

Wayne: Throwing of lumps o' coal, and you can't see a lump o' coal coming when it's dark. It was awkward for me because my dad worked for the Coal Board in Chesterfield and quite a lot o' my family did. I used to go out onto the pits out there and sometime, in the line of pickets, would be people that I'd been at school with, relatives and people that knew me because of me dad - really awkward for me, but I didn't get any bother, not from them anyway. It was mainly the flying pickets.

Most enjoyable points

Wayne: Most enjoyable was just basically working me patch, getting to know people, going into the schools, giving a talk to the children about different things, perhaps taking an assembly, knowing people in the village, all the different characters in the place; there's very rarely it was boring. Having a cup o' tea and a natter. It certainly wasn't a bad place to work; it was grand.

Paul: You'd probably get something that was a bit stronger than a cup o' tea depending where you was as well, which is a no-no now. Joe Hutchinson, the farmer; if you called on Joe for anything, the whisky bottle jumped out of the cupboard before you sat down! But woe betide you if you went in smellin' of the stuff to certain officers!

Wayne: I didn't drink, but Joe'd slip me a few in me coffee, like, when we're sheep dippin'. Once there'd bin a couple o' days where he'd done it to me and I said, "Joe, I hope you don't mind, I've got a bit of a queasy tummy, I'd better not". "I've got just the thing," he said, and he came back with hot milk laced with whisky! - for me tummy! Lovely fellow! I used to enjoy the sheep-dipping and cattle movements, mixing with the farmers. That was good.

Amusing memories

Chemist's roof

Wayne: There was that incident about the chemist's and the flat roof. There's a wall with a flat roof and then there's the chemist's. Well that flat roof was how they broke into the chemist's once before. So the chemist had asked me about alarms and stuff like this. So I give him advice and then I said, "Well if there's going to be a delay between getting the stuff fitted, put some anti-climb paint on that wall and on that flat roof" - It's greasy stuff- it's dreadful – "At least you'll stop 'em from climbing up there."

Well about a week later, the alarm went off at the chemist's so all the officers turned out and I turned up on my bike, and I said to 'em, "It's all right, I know how they broke in last time, I'll go and have a look on that flat roof." So up I went on this wall, up onto this flat roof – suddenly realised I was covered in anti- climb paint! It was on me hands, me tunic, even on the end of me nose! And I stood there, I couldn't get it off, with me arms out, and the key-holder of the chemist turned up and he looked at me and he said, "Oh, it works then, does it?!"

School break-in

Wayne: (Shelton Lock School was) broken into one night. We got the caretaker, old Fred Warren, down. Had a look round. The alarm panel was showing fault, so we weren't really looking too hard. We checked all the outside windows and couldn't find anything. The place all looked secure. On the right hand side near the door was the caretaker's broom cupboard. We set the alarms again and as everyone was going out, I opened it and had a look in. Shut it again. We locked up. I stood outside, and I suddenly realised that there was somebody in there! It hadn't registered. So we went back in and this lad is still in there - he'd not had time to do anything. Later he said, "Didn't you see me?" Just stood in the broom cupboard!

Fancy dress

Wayne: Don Prime (lived at what is now "The Bonnie Prince"). We checked his premises a lot – he had some really important guests. I'd got to be in the house with his guests at a party – fancy dress. So I got a Captain Pugwash suit. There were a lot of important politicians, nice vehicles and Captain Pugwash looked after them!

Don Prime's house – now the "Bonnie Prince"

Ukrainian Centre

Wayne: Paul'd got the panda car at the time. I was due to meet up with him, take the panda car off him to continue my patrol the next day, but we decided to nip into the Ukranian camp (at Weston-on-Trent). I used to have a lot to do with them down there. We parked the police car and walked down the track to the club house. All the old Ukrainian chaps were in there from the wartime, having a drink and we were invited in – roaring log fire.

We'd bin in there a few minutes when this little old chap came in and whispered something to the others and somebody came up to us and said, "There's an officer coming down the track to the club!" Well, that meant it was one of our inspectors or somebody like that so Paul and I shot out the back door, scrambled up through the wood, got in the panda car, cleared off and went and signed off duty.

We found out later that this inspector burst into the place - which quite honestly he'd no right to because it was a private club – and said, "Right, where's the officers?" And two or three of these little old Ukrainian chaps stood up and saluted him and said, "Ei... am... ze... offizer!" Nobody told him that we'd been in there!

More serious memories of career

Paul: I dealt with a straight-up sudden death of a baby. I went to the Children's Hospital, into the morgue. This baby was on its back on a purple cushion. Quite upsetting to see a young baby taken like that.

(Another) one that comes to mind: about 10 past 10 we got called to the Cambridge Hotel at night time in the early seventies – a mass murder there, a racial thing between the Pakistanis and the Indians. Probably half a dozen being attacked or murdered. You couldn't see the horrificness of it until the following morning. It was just like a slaughter house where all the bodies had slaumed along and left a trademark of blood trails. Yes, quite horrific. That's stayed with me.

Wayne: The most horrific thing I was involved in was a 3 year old girl that was taken, murdered off Sinfin Lane. We searched all night; the whole estate turned out to help us in freezing fog. The body was found in the vicarage garden, Browning St. That took some getting over.

If you'd have gone back to the station saying, "I'm having nightmares about this", you'd have been told, "If you can't stand (the heat) better get out of the kitchen – out of the job". That one took me years to get over because my kids were the same age.

Later career

Wayne: (I moved to Little Chester). I was walking through the Market Place on night shift one night at 2am with a young bobby I was training. There was a gang of football hooligans. This bobby went into the middle of the gang to sort them and they beat him up. I'd got to get him out. I got beaten up very badly (but) I took a few of them down with me. I ended up with 2 neck bones dislocated and they damaged my diaphragm. My health went downhill and I still suffer.

(I then became) Station Enquiry Officer in the Market Place (dealing with) lost and found purses, bus-drivers' accidents, directions. The station has tinted glass – we can see out but they can't see in. One of the funniest things is, before young ladies go into the Assembly Rooms, they used to straighten their attire, pick spots and we're on the other side!

POLICE – NOW

PCSO Chris Wright and PC Jim Palmer

PCSO Chris Wright

PC Jim Palmer

Early days

Chris Wright, Police Community Support Officer (PCSO)

I was born in Norwich in 1979. My family still live back in Norfolk, my father is an accountant, my mother works for the royal family at Sandringham.

I went to do a BSc Honours Environmental Sciences degree at the University of East Anglia. I moved to Derby working at the police headquarters in Ripley in a department called geographical information systems which was related to my degree - using digital mapping. In the police we used it for plotting crime statistics, planning routes of where people had moved, where cars had moved, chases and that sort of thing. I did that for 3 years.

Jim Palmer, Police Constable (PC)

I was born in 1976 in Derby. My mother and father were both catering managers until later in life. Then my father was a bus driver for his last years.

I attended schools in Melbourne where I grew up. Then I came to Chellaston School. I went to Wilmorton College where I did a BTech National, which was in Business Management and from there I went to Loughborough College and did Higher National Diploma, in business studies. Then I was based at Warrington, part of Manchester University, where I completed my degree prior to joining this job.

Joining the Police

Chris (PCSO)

The role of a PCSO is being more in the community, meeting and speaking to people, a high visibility presence. They are still a new idea, I believe they came in 6 maybe 7 years ago. It is a separate role to the PC (and) attracts people from different backgrounds. We don't have so much paperwork to do: we don't get involved with taking statements and the more serious crimes, we don't arrest people. Obviously when somebody is arrested it's quite a lot of paperwork that needs to be filled out and that's time that's taking PCs off the streets. We don't have as many forms to fill in. We are out and about more. We spend 70-80% of our time on the streets being seen, being visible, dealing with more low level issues and getting a better feel for the community and what problems are facing it.

PCSOs work as part of a Safer Neighbourhood Team probably 1 PCSO to 1PC. There are about 110-120 (of us) covering Derby town centre and South Derbyshire. In Chellaston there are 3 PCSOs and 2PCs. People have said that they see PCSOs as a more traditional style beat officer in that they know all the problems, know where to go when somebody has had eggs thrown at the window. They know who's going to be the main culprits because they've got that better knowledge of the area.

The academic qualifications you need are 5 GCSEs, grades A to C, some colleagues have degrees but its more your life experience, personality and how you deal with conflict. A lot of that's picked up during the interview and assessment stages. I don't believe there is a fitness test as such. There is a medical assessment to make sure that you could bend, jump up and down - flexibility.

I applied to be a PCSO rather than staring at a computer which is what I spent most of my old job doing. There were no vacancies for PCs at that time - Derbyshire police only really take on for very short periods, probably once a year maybe every other year. There's such a large number of people apply, they don't need to keep the recruitment window open for long. I saw this role as being the ideal way of seeing what it was all about and getting a background as to what PCs did. Some 4 years on, I realise that this is more what I want to do.

Jim (PC)

I grew up hearing about the police from family. It was always seen in high esteem. My great grandfather was an inspector in the police force in Lincolnshire. I've still got a set of his original handcuffs. It's changed completely from what he told me at the time. There's a lot of things he could deal with (at) his own discretion, from start to finish, there and then on the street, where obviously things (now) are a bit different. I've got two cousins who are police officers (Their) job satisfaction rolled on to me.

I applied for the police force at the time I graduated. It was basically in stages to join. It started with the written exams, then a formal interview process then physical and medical exam. I'm not sure of the actual formal qualifications. There's no restriction on height any more. If you come in as a graduate, there is a high potential scheme - you can progress through the ranks at a speedier rate. A high number come in as graduates.

Training

Chris (PCSO)

We were at Ripley Headquarters for 6 weeks, (learning) different parts of the law, how to deal with conflict in situations. There was a section on first aid, self-defence, personal safety. You spend half a day in the control room. (Doing your job) you do spend a lot of your day on the radio to a voice in a control room, so it's nice to know what they do. We also go to Magistrate's Court for half a day - there are times when we have to go to court and give evidence. 2 weeks of those 6 you go out to the station where you'll be based so that you can get more of a feel for the area you'll be working. Then you can bring these questions back to the Assessor, to iron out any problems.

When you get deployed to your area, you get mentored for 4 weeks (until) you're deemed to be OK to be patrolling the streets on your own; you're not going to walk into a situation and put yourself in danger and not create or make a situation worse.

Jim (PC)

If someone was to join the police today the training is in-house up at Ripley H.Q. When I joined the job, coming up for 11 years ago, it was Bruche training camp up in Cheshire. I studied at a satellite campus at Warrington Uni for about 4 months. Up at 8 o'clock. We would have a parade outside our residential block in full uniform - check that your boots were polished, shirts ironed etc. Then we would do drill practice, very similar to the army. Then we would spend the morning doing some classroom exercises: they'd go through a lot of the law - very in-depth training on traffic law, criminal damage, law of assault and then scenarios within that. Then you would do a test.

In the afternoon (we did) physical exercise or self-defence training. We also did a life-saving certificate. The campus had mock roads - they'd set up scenes of accidents etc. or they'd set up a public order affray in one of the halls, which we'd deal with. Because you had to stay away, everybody gelled - one big family really.

In self-defence (we learned) a lot of take-down moves (for) if you are in a violent situation, how to take the person down to the ground and lots of handcuff techniques, and baton training. You do have to be fit but it is also up to the individual as to how much you contribute to that. We do a self-defence course each year – you have to be up to date with your self-defence - but there's no actual test of your physical fitness. I don't really have any concerns because I have always liked to keep on top of my own fitness.

We did C.S. gas training: we would line up on the field outside and someone would come down and spray the line with the C.S. gas and you'd walk into the cloud of C.S. and see the effect it would have on you. (It was) quite severe. I wear contact lenses so I could feel my eyes burning up. You just want to wet your face but if you dampen your face or rub your eyes it has even more effect. As it dries it crystallises so you can feel it in your hair. Yes, very good stuff.

Once you have done that training you come to a station rather than a beat. I don't think you fully appreciate or fully get to grips with things until you are in the situation of being out on the streets. At the time I joined you are with a tutor constable for a period of 10 weeks. I knew this area better than any other area. I put it (as my) preference.

Cotton Lane was where I was based initially. Everyone had their own seats. One chap had done about 20 years service at Cotton. My first day at work I can remember sitting in his seat and being picked up under both arms and moved to the side and then being told the first job is to make a cup of tea! That's how it started but I was very welcomed. My first arrest was for non-payment of a fine warrant - on Chellaston Road further down in Allenton. I can remember Paul saying to me, "Right, first thing we are going to do is knock on this door, chap by the name of such and such, he's got an outstanding payment of fines warrant." Knocked on the door, big chap answered and I thought, "Crikey!" and he was as compliant as anything to be fair to the chap. Within an hour of my shift I was sat next to him in the back of the police car. Now we don't execute non-payment of fines warrants – they go out to a private company. That was a baptism of fire straight away which was quite nice.

After you have been with your tutor constable you go back and do a driving course to make sure you are able to drive the police car - you can use your blue lights etc. I had just become independent from my tutor and it was about 5 o'clock in the morning; we were doing night shifts at the time, we did 7 at night to 7 in the morning, and we were doing paperwork. Manjit, the sergeant, said, "Do you fancy a cup of tea?" I said, "Yes, I'd love a cup of tea." He said, "There's only one thing, you'll have to take the car out for the first time and get some milk." So I went out to get some milk. Coming through from Allenton down towards Shelton Lock, there is a car in front of me, a black VW. There just seemed something not quite right about it. I followed it at a safe distance and as it recognised I was a police car it started to speed off, so I shouted on my radio, "There's a car making off!" and read the registration plate out.

I followed the car and I can remember from my training my trainer saying, "If you do ever stop a car with various occupants in, the most important person to get is the driver because more offences have been committed." Lo and behold, they all star-burst out of the car, both back doors opened, both front doors opened. I went straight for the driver. He tried to climb over a wall; he was a very heavy built chap and we detained him. It came out that the car had actually been taken from a car key burglary in Bradford. They had been (involved in) a series of burglaries. Now, a lot of chases are aborted unless it is a traffic officer pursuing, due to health and safety issues.

Uniform and equipment

Chris (PCSO)

(We have) standard black trousers the same as PCs. White shirt. We wear a blue tie, PCs wear a black tie. They have a black fleece with a sort of blue and white chequered band; ours has "Police Community Support Officer" on rather than just "Police." We have the blue epaulettes on our shoulders as opposed to black. Our hats - the main difference - ours are flat, cap style (with) a blue band around; PCs' more of the old fashioned and traditional hat.

Main equipment: we don't have handcuffs or CS gas or a baton, but from a distance, everything else probably looks quite similar. We have a stab or slash-proof vest and an equipment carrier vest which we can attach our radio to, our mobile data device. Things like fixed penalty tickets, pocket notebook. (Our) stab- proof vest is more up to date now; it's a lot more lightweight, thinner. I believe it's Kevlar material, more comfortable in Summer and doesn't restrict your movement at all. It is up to you if you wear a stab vest or not, however I've been doing it for 4 years and even in the hottest days in Summer I've always worn it. It's better to be safe than sorry, I think. I think if you were stabbed it does penetrate probably about an inch - it doesn't let the knife through but you do still feel it. In 4 years I've never come across a situation where I'm glad I was wearing it, but you never know. Someone who was in my intake of PCSOs was allocated a town north of Derbyshire and within her first 2 weeks of being mentored came across an armed robbery.

You have to buy your own boots - they're just standard, black patrol boots. I must have been through about 6 pairs in 4 years. Before we had a base at Chellaston in June last year, we were walking from Cotton Lane down to Chellaston at least once maybe twice a day, plus the miles you would be patrolling around Chellaston. So we were easily walking 15-20 miles a day.

Jim (PC)

(I wear the same uniform) throughout the year. The only difference you will see today is I have got some cycling trousers on. I work between Chellaston and Shelton Lock and I have to get back to the main station at times – Cotton Lane. I cycle back there so I can use the main computer terminals, so I've got my cycling kit on for that which is slightly more lightweight, but still very warm throughout the summer.

As a PC on the beat or on section the helmet (is) still the very traditional helmet shape. It's quite weighty. The difference between ourselves and the PCSOs is that they have the flat caps. In Derbyshire the only people who get the flat caps are inspectors or traffic section. In other forces you get flat caps.

You can either wear a vest carrier, which they started issuing a couple of years ago, or the traditional belt. The belt rides up and down and becomes quite uncomfortable (so) I've got a vest carrier on, which I choose because I do a lot of walking on the beat. It carries all the instruments and apparatus we carry around and CS gas on a hold-all with an elasticated strip which allows me to direct the CS gas. I would say it would reach 10ft away from you. In eleven years service I have used it 3 times. One time in Derby city centre that was used on 2 individuals outside a pub prior to arrest - a large amount of disorder. You have to tell them "I am going to deploy CS gas, stand back." At that point I drew the CS spray; they continued to advance towards me so I sprayed the CS gas. They went down. They became very calm after that. They were put in the back of the carrier. You try to isolate them from the rest of the people because coming into contact you are going to get the reaction yourself as well. If I come in contact with it, with my hands, you have to be very careful where you are putting your hands then.

Another time, I detained someone who was wanted for a theft from a motor vehicle down in Allenton. He decided to make off from us and hid under a lorry down in Ascot Drive. He wouldn't come out; he grabbed hold of the lorry and was kicking out. I warned him that we were going to deploy CS gas. We deployed the CS and at that point he was able to let go from under the lorry. We removed him and he was detained. The third and final time was for some public order, again on a back street in Allenton, after a community event. A shop window had been put through. It had escalated further and further and one individual wouldn't calm down. He wouldn't listen to us. We couldn't get the handcuffs on him because he was so out of control. I have heard of some individuals it does not affect whatsoever, but I have not come across that myself. Obviously, after that you have to go to the extendable baton – you flick it out - into 2 ratchet areas. To put it back down you have to hit it very hard on a solid surface. That can have a longer term effect depending on which body part you strike. CS gas is most beneficial in a lot of situations really.

Underneath this vest you have got the body armour which is obviously ballistic- proof - it prevents any bullets or stabs.   Every time I come on duty it goes on and it comes off at the end of the shift. It gets unbearable to be honest.   During the summer months very, very warm. It does come down to choice but obviously if something were to happen to myself or another officer and you weren't wearing that you would leave yourself wide open, so best practice is that that you wear it. If you were on an operation such as football duty or coming out with a warrant on an address or at any briefing, the sergeant would say," Ensure you have got full protective kit on at all times." I have never come under attack from a weapon; however you could go to any job at any time.   I could go to a violent domestic incident where the nearest thing in a kitchen, where they are talking to me, is a rack of knives. I've never known anyone stabbed. Officers have been attacked by other means: a colleague of mine had taken a prisoner down to the cells in the city centre and the female turned round and bit him; he'd got permanent damage caused to his hand.

(We) don't get a boot allowance now. The officer is left to choose their own boots. I know the vast percentage of police officers will use Hi-Tech Magnums. I probably get through 2 pairs of these a year. They are comfortable, as far as boots go.

We have the handcuffs, which are the standard pair of handcuffs that we hold. As soon as I place them on someone's wrist it will flip round, open up and clasp onto the wrist and the handcuff key will lock the cuffs in place. We never ever join ourselves onto a detained person.

We have some leg restraints.   They are on my belt.   They are basically 2 long strips, one side Velcro and if you are unable to lift anyone up or get them into the desired place, you wrap them round the legs and another one further up and it completely puts them under your control to move them into the van or the car.

Normally in this pouch there would be a First Aid kit and some gloves - a resuscitation aid, just in case I need to resuscitate anybody, a protection mouth aid for me.

We've got the radio which has changed dramatically since I joined.   It's basically a bulky mobile phone used to send messages. It is used on what we call an Air Wave. When I am talking on this Air Wave we've got 2 operators at the call centre at Ripley taking the calls and they are passing the dialogue onto us over the Air Wave.   I can hear what they are saying to any other officer and I can also hear what the other officer is saying back to the person.

When I first joined the job, the radio was far bigger, I'd say another 50% on top of this and the battery was half the radio. Nothing digital on it - it was a closed air wave - you could only hear what the operator was saying you couldn't hear what any other officer was saying. This is open so we can hear what is going on all the time and on top of that the channel can be changed so I could go on and listen to what is happening in the city centre or Peartree. There is an orange button. If an officer presses the orange button that goes through to the Communications room; it would also send a message through to me. It will continually make a noise like an alarm noise in my ear saying someone's in bother and the air wave will open up just to that person and the operator until we know what has happened. Then they'd clear that air wave and we would make our way towards them.

I always carry round my standard torch. Next to that is what they call a PDA which is a small computer really. This has on it all the incidents. I have a unique number. Our Control room is called Oscar 2, so if Oscar 2 shouted, "Delta 998, I need you to attend an address down in Shelton Lock." I'd say, "Could you pass me the incident number." Type this into there - it will give me the dialogue of who's called the incident in. In the header it will tell me the job description, tell me what's been done on the job so far, then I'll go into that and I can update it from there.

PCSO Chris Wright

PC Jim Palmer

A typical day's work in Chellaston

Chris (PCSO)

I probably start 5 out of my 6 days, at the base we have at the rear of Chellaston Library. It has a separate access so that we can use it 24 hours a day. It's got our lockers down here so that we can have our uniform and equipment rather than needing to go back to Cotton Lane so often.

We tend to come and go from here. If we're here, if anyone wants to speak to us they can just ask a member of the library staff who will usually just come and knock on the door and we'll go and speak to them. There's 2 desks that we use for paperwork, a CS gas canister holder for the 2 PCs and a smaller desk so that members of the public and youngsters that may need to come in to discuss their behaviour, can come and speak to us.

We also hold our monthly police surgeries in here - we've got 4 chairs, various whiteboards for meetings, forums. We've a large map of the area and a police bike. It's got a pannier bag on the back, that's got a water bottle, forms, fixed penalty notices in it. (It has a) high powered battery unit for the lights - we can use that to search areas at night time. We have 2 police bikes down here; it's a really good way for us to get around - obviously more enjoyable in the summer.

We work (either) 8 o'clock till 4, 10 o'clock until 6, 12 till 8 or 2 till 10. If we started at 8 o'clock we would get in, get kitted up - our stab vest on, our equipment carrier and then go straight out. That time of the day the children are starting school. We patrol around the schools when we can, it's obviously the issues of children's safety, and also parking around a lot of the schools with parents dropping their kids off near the gates. If somebody's parked and they're blocking the road or the yellow zig-zag making it dangerous for the children, difficult for people to see, then we'll advise them to move on. If they are obstructing a driveway or blocking the road completely then we can issue tickets. Some schools have greater parking problems - it's very difficult for us to solve these on a long term basis.

Last week I went to Homefields School on Parkway to speak to some year 6 children about "stranger danger", (and) about how to cross the road safely. One of the things that was touched on was (if) you've got your head in your mobile phone, your MP3 player in, listening to music, being safe crossing the road perhaps isn't your highest priority at that time. Mobile phones and MP3 players are obviously quite valuable, so you've also got the sort of personal safety aspect there for the children.

We have a patrol strategy which is the areas that have been affected by crime. We can be passed incidents from the control room which could be anything from nuisance youths, checking on a vulnerable, elderly person, it could be a follow up visit for a car crime or a burglary, a neighbour dispute between 2 addresses. We do have a beat mobile that we carry round with us. It is given to shops and things like that – it's more of a direct access to whoever's on duty, if they just want us to pop in because they've had a problem. We've also all been issued with mobile data devices which we can carry around with us which we can access e-mails on, view incidents and also do person and vehicle checks on.

In the last few years, policing has gone back to more on a local level – having a specific beat team responsible for a small area. People – (especially) elderly people - often don't call the police because they don't want to waste our time, so by being more approachable and more human, people talk to us more openly, rather than not telling us about things that are happening.

Jim (PC)

Our beat goes as far as where the Bonnie Prince estate is, it cuts off there, and then we go as far as Merrill Way, where the allotments are. The Local Intelligence Officer at Cotton Lane puts the briefing together: he views all crimes that happen in Derby East section and he will do an overview of what's happened in those areas. From that he will pick hot spots. When I book on duty the Communications Room will tell me that there are a certain amount of anti-social behaviour jobs. Say I come on duty at 2, I will have on average four incidents a day. I work through it. Then I have got my priorities - we have a Neighbourhood Forum every quarter; at that 3 priorities are set; we work at that until the next Forum.

I have two different days' work: either come on duty at the Library - where we are based as a sub-station – and self-brief myself (from) briefing documents from the Local Intelligence Officer. Alternatively, I book on duty at Cotton Lane, sit down in a formal briefing run by the shift sergeant; he will go through a list of what's happened over the last week, who's wanted etc. A separate data base has got all our crime incidents on, so I have got my incidents, my crimes and any info that has come my way. Then I'll walk on the beat being a high visibility presence, also going to priority areas, dealing with all the incidents that have come in overnight or during the week. As I come out of the Library I'd look for any pockets of anti-social behaviour, any groups, any gatherings. I'd try to engage with the groups as well. There are hard to reach groups – people who do not want to engage with the police. They'd be very standoffish because of previous instances or perception of the police, but I'd still try and integrate with them to get information from them and feed from that.

In Chellaston (I) look for any areas I know there are vulnerable people living. Everything all right in those areas, any insecurities? Due to auto car offences in the area, I would be looking for any property left on show in cars. I'd check the vehicle and I would send a letter to the keeper just to raise awareness in the area. I'm looking all the time, any motoring offences, any out of date tax disc displayed - very minor things but also things that can paint a bigger picture. If I came out of the Library today, I would have a walk down Station Road around (St.) David's Close area. I'd then come back up. It used to be an area of anti-social behaviour round the back of the Corner Pin so I'd still have a walk down there.

At the bottom of Station Road we'd go in (St.) David's Close. A percentage of individuals try to use a short cut over some residential gardens to get on the Bonnie Prince estate. I'm actively trying to ascertain who those individuals are. I then come back up and I'd go up the High Street, visit the shops, speak to the local businesses, check how things have been. I'd walk through the churchyard and the cemetery and then round to Back Lane and Pit Close. I'd come back across towards Fellowlands.   Try to cover as many of the streets I can and then come down onto Back Lane and through back on to Maple Drive. I'd continue down to Shelton Lock, join onto the canal path, then come back round on Sinfin Avenue, join back onto the other side of the canal path and then come down to West Avenue North where there's a cut through to the Bonnie Prince estate, weaving in and out those streets, down onto Rowallan Way, cut past the Bonnie Prince, back down Swarkestone Road and I'd be back in the centre of Chellaston. We cover an average 25 to 30 kilometres a day on foot.

Plenty of residents will offer me a cup of tea when I'm out and about. I'd say any business I could walk into in Chellaston and they'd say, "Jim, do you want a cup of tea? Help yourself to a cup of tea." It's nice to build rapport with people.

Since we've had the Library – fantastic! - I would say 90% of the time is spent on the beat.   Prior to that, you'd waste a good 3 hours of the day just walking backwards and forwards from Cotton Lane. Once you have self- briefed yourself you are out of the door, nip back for your lunch for 15 mins, and back out. I finish my duty at 8 o'clock this evening. I shall be out until 7-30 unless anything major happens. I aim to get back in to de-kit, mark off any jobs I've come across and make myself a list of what I need to do when I go back to the main police station at some point tomorrow to update the other systems. That's a typical sort of day.

Anti-social behaviour

Chris (PCSO)

There are a couple of locations in Chellaston where groups of youths will gather: at the moment our main problem is around the One Stop and George's area on Rowallan Way. We have a lot of calls regarding large groups down there - probably between 30 and 40 - so obviously we try and get down there as much as we can. They're not committing any crimes as such but just by virtue of the size of the group its making people feel intimidated - puts people off going into the shops. If we then move them from the front of the shops they go onto the park across the road. People living near that park are being kept awake at night by 30 children shouting and screaming. So obviously we're working at the moment to try and solve that problem. I must say Chellaston has grown a great deal in size and bringing that extra number of children to the area without probably the facilities to deal with them has brought about this problem.

The shopping area in Rowallan Way.

They'll always say from their point of view they're not doing anything wrong, they're just hanging around with their friends. We try and educate them that perhaps outside shops and people's houses isn't the best place to congregate. But then they'll reply that there is nothing for us to do in Chellaston. But that's something else we're trying to work on at the moment, working with various youth groups, youth services, councillors, all different people to try to get some activities into Chellaston for the children to do. You do build - I wouldn't say a friendship or a relationship - but you get this rapport with them.

Jim (PC)

Being a beat officer, anti-social behaviour and long term issues is my bread and butter. We tackle unsocial behaviour in a positive way. The businesses have got regular contacts with ourselves. We've put a camera in place at Rowallan Way, (and have) carried out an operation where every Friday and Saturday night we will have at least 4 officers, Youth Service and a police van, mobiles down there. Anyone who has committed anti-social behaviour, we place on an Acceptable Behaviour Contract, whereby they come into Cotton Lane, sit down with their parents and we work through a voluntary set of guidelines towards acceptable behaviour.

Different parents react in different ways. (The) majority of parents are very supportive of us. Some are of the opinion that there is nothing for the youth to do. I categorically say there are a number of things to do in Chellaston. There is a Youth Club that has been set up for the younger element. There are things run each evening from the Senior School – a tremendous amount of work goes on there trying to put things in place. We've had about 10 individuals in to Cotton Lane police station. Out of those 10 we have now got 6 on ABCs where they come back to the police station every month. We go through what their behaviour has been like for the last month - from what we've come across as police officers, what the parents have said. The school come along to the meeting.

There's still a percentage who hang about down there - we monitor the camera to see what they are doing. It's quality of life and if the sheer volume is preventing someone going into a shop then it's still an issue. We work with One Stop and George's; the businesses have got regular contact with ourselves and there's been a massive improvement during the time this has been put in place. Every time I am on duty I make sure I go down to check what it has been like, make them aware I am on duty at whatever time.

Traffic offences/ incidents

Chris (PCSO)

We've had operations in Chellaston whereby we've had people who've been parked up further down the road who identify drivers who've been on their mobile phones or not wearing their seat belts. Then they've been pulled over a short distance down the road and issued with tickets. Unfortunately it's not something that PCSOs can give a ticket for, and we don't have the power to stop the vehicle. However, if there is a driver on a mobile phone stopped in traffic then there have been several times when we would give them some words of advice and they've always got off their phone.

Chellaston has got the 7.5 ton weight limit. Before the Red Lion was being developed into Tesco's it was an ideal place for us to pull lorries over. We had an operation every couple of months where probably 6 or 7 police officers and PCSOs along with Trading Standards pulled every lorry over that came through Chellaston that was overweight. Then it was either given a fixed penalty ticket or if Trading Standards found anything else then they were dealt with for that. Word gets around to all the other drivers not to use Chellaston as a short cut. If a lorry has got legitimate access within the area then it's fine to use the road.

Myself and another colleague have stood outside the Library and pulled them over because the road is just about wide enough to not cause traffic chaos.

If I was first on the scene (of an accident), I would do as much as a PC would do. We've all had the same training – obviously some have had it in more depth; if a traffic officer arrived, he's had more training with that. But we'd still be able to assess the scene, try and figure out if there's any first aid we could give unless we're putting ourselves in danger.

First thing we'd do is create an "incident" with the control room to get some more people here if the road needs closing. Give details, a brief overview of what's happened and then if anyone was at fault and a prosecution needed doing, we would do a statement of our initial account and if there are any offences then, obviously another officer would follow that up.

PCSO Chris Wright and his police cycle.

A few months ago I was involved with a slight accident. I wasn't badly injured, but it took a few days to get back into .... I was on a push bike on the canal path. There was a moped with two lads on, coming towards me. They looked like they were going to stop, but they didn't, they carried on and we hit head on. They were on a moped going about 25-30 miles an hour and I was on a push bike, practically stationary. I fell off, they fell off. I'd hurt my leg, but then they got on their moped and rode off. I was laying on the floor with a bike on top of me so It was quite difficult. I got the registration of the bike (which) was later found dumped somewhere.

Jim (PC)

An incident (not in Chellaston) that sticks in my mind (was) where a fight spilled out from a pub onto the Spider Island at Allenton. I had to go down to the pub and there was a pizza delivery man coming down the road. He hit one of the people who had been fighting; the person went straight over. The pizza delivery driver continued to drive (with) the chap trapped under the vehicle. I was one of the first officers on the scene and the chap was taken to hospital. He survived with very, very minor injuries. That just absolutely amazed me. The trauma the body had been through – quite incredible really.

One night we saw a person we knew was a disqualified driver come from the end of Shelton Lock into the Peartree area and we pursued him. It was really icy. We'd lost our vision on him for a little period of time. He'd stopped the vehicle and just as we came round the corner he was going round to the passenger side and his wife to the driver's side and they continued to drive off. The female was trying to make away from us and due to the ice on the road she collided with some parked vehicles and we managed to detain the chap. He still continued to deny the fact that he had been driving the vehicle when we had clearly seen the switchover. He was later sentenced in Court. He went all the way to Court denying everything.

PC Jim Palmer at the corner of Station Rd and Derby Rd, Chellaston

Police helicopter

Chris (PCSO)

Last time I was involved with the police helicopter was (when) there were quite a few nuisance motor bikes on Weston Fields at the back of Ridgeway, using that as a track. That has been a problem on and off since I started. There are so many entrances and exits off that area that it's impossible for us to corner them. It is the first time from memory it's been over for the motor bikes.

Other occasions it's been (used) because there is a missing child, (or) elderly people who've gone missing that we've not managed to locate. It is usually used for tracking criminals, people who have fled off from us or cars have made off.

Jim (PC)

We've had the use of the helicopter quite a lot in Chellaston. We had 2 young missing girls who had made their way from Chellaston back down to Derby, travelled quite a significant distance and at that time we used the force helicopter. That was very good because they used the tannoy from the helicopter and sent out community messages as to the description of the girls that were missing and the amount of calls we had from using that was phenomenal. Within the hour the girls had been found which was excellent really.

Other problems, crimes in Chellaston/Shelton Lock area

Chris (PCSO)

When I first started here in the Summer 4 years ago we were having quite a few problems with groups from Alvaston and Allenton coming over to have these pre-arranged fights with Chellaston children - some of them having sticks, baseball bats, that sort of thing. This hasn't happened for the last 3 years.

There's not been a huge spate of burglaries or car crime; obviously we do get a few.

Jim (PC)

There's a very small minority, pocket of individuals that commit crime in Chellaston area I would say. When they are active crime obviously goes through the roof. It's getting the evidence to prove it's the individuals. We will actively seek intelligence on those individuals at that time. There are travelling criminals in any area.

There is no major problem with drugs at Chellaston. We do get intelligence regarding the use of drugs in the area. As soon as intelligence is gathered, it is acted upon extremely quickly with the execution of warrants. It does go on - nobody's naive to say there aren't people using drugs but I would say in Chellaston the drugs being used (or) have been used are more cannabis related.

We deal with a fair few neighbour disputes. A lot of satisfaction comes from those. We've solved some long standing disputes. Numerous times when I've knocked on the door the person's said, "I knew that was a police officer" so you've got the policeman's knock! There was one that was going on for a couple of years. It all stemmed from fall-out by children, then escalates to the parents. There was a lot of abuse being shouted at each individual as they came out of the house and a lot of noise from adjoining properties. We hired the Community Centre and sat down with a mediation company, and we ironed out the differences between both parties. I still visit the people now. It's amazing to see: for a number of years there had been so much animosity towards each other and now they are happily getting on about their business with each other.

We had an upsurge in car crime across the whole of D division that spiralled down into Chellaston, Shelton Lock and there was a lot of theft from vehicles etc. in Chellaston. Fortunately, we detained somebody for that. A resident of Chellaston found some footprints in the snow. As a beat team we managed to track down the footsteps. The person was arrested and subsequently admitted over a hundred car offences in the area of Chellaston/Shelton Lock and also in Derby.

The results they get with DNA is second to none. I'd been to the scene of a burglary in Shelton Lock and at the scene of the burglary was a cigarette butt, still smoking – just a nub end. I seized that cigarette butt and that was sent off for SOCO analysis - they took DNA from the cigarette butt. From that we traced (and) arrested the offender. Twenty months later he failed to turn up at Court. We came back through Allenton, saw the male who had failed to turn up at Court and he ran like a greyhound over walls, over fences. I jumped over a wall, fell over the next fence, went over a wheelie bin, fell over and I found him hiding behind a shed at the bottom of the garden. You have to be athletic at times! It's awfully rewarding when you come back with them in the cuffs.

Changes to duties

Jim (PC)

You get a change of duty when you have to cover events and football duties. You either get a cancelled rest day or they'll take me from this area of Chellaston. It's a change of scenery, a different sort of policing. I used to be public order trained. I'm quite a big football fan so that's one of the reasons I enjoy policing them, although you don't get the chance to watch it - it's the atmosphere. (In) recent years the violence at a football match is, I would say, reduced significantly. Certain matches, such as Derby against Forest, or Derby against Leicester are very heavily policed from the point of the train station, the public houses the home fans drink in, away fans drink in. There are police officers with hand held cameras gathering intelligence on these individuals – where they're going. They are chaperoned to the football matches, contained within the match and escorted away out of Derby. So I would have said disorder at football matches, from my point of view, is minimal. If you were working at a football match, there's a lot of emergency planning they go through in a briefing situation.

Hazards/emergencies/sudden death

Jim (PC)

If you are the first one (on the scene), you have to establish control, notify the Control Room exactly what is going on, notify the supervisor and establish whether any cordons needed. Towards the back end of Shelton Lock, I can remember a chap who had found an old hand grenade in his back garden. We were first there and we had to cordon off the street and everyone had to come out their properties. We were waiting for messages from the Control Room and for Bomb Disposal to come.

I've been to a lot of sudden deaths or suspicious deaths where someone has been found deceased we take our enquiries from there. I can remember one chap we'd gone along to and he was actually found in the bath. I was the first officer there.
You switch off from it, distance yourself. It's part of your job. You do your job and you leave the scene. (But) it's always there in your mind. After I had been to that particular job I'd got back to the station a couple of hours later to have my corned beef sandwiches and I could still smell the situation I had been in. I've never had a corned beef sandwich since until literally last week. But I had some last week. I rang my wife and said, "Could you just pick some corned beef up? I just feel like bringing some corned beef sandwiches this week to work."

When I joined the job I thought one of the things I would find most difficult (would be) to pass on information which I knew was going to cause an enormous amount of grief to that person. I've had to do it and it doesn't get any easier no matter how many times you do it because that information affects someone's life for ever. It's not a nice experience. Unfortunately, it's part and parcel of the job. However many times you do it, it still brings a lot of emotions.

Rewards of the job

Chris (PCSO)

I do like the job. It's nice to be able to come into work and not be stuck in an office all day. It's what you make it: I like trying to speak to as many people as I can. I like to be known in the area. You'll go to addresses and it's nice for them to say, "Yes, I've seen you walking around a lot." It's nice to solve a problem that somebody's been having, and get to the bottom of it, and for them to be grateful and appreciate it at the end of it. It gives you personal satisfaction.

Jim (PC)

To get a full pension you do 30 years' service. If I manage to do my 30 years' service, I'll be 54 when I retire. I think you can retire after 25 years' service on a reduced pension. A lot used to stay on – there was a scheme called 30+ Scheme when an officer could stay on, be offered a year-on-year rolling contract. A lot of them would be office jobs - become a civilian but have the same sort of responsibility. I think that was on a reduced wage, but I believe that's gone. Others go into the security side of things or some sort of part time job.

What satisfies me is restoring someone's quality of life. Especially in the role of Safer Neighbourhood Officer, the fact that some people I come to see have been dealing with things from month to month, from years to years, whether it's from a neighbour dispute or whether it's gangs of youths causing them problems. When you have got to the bottom of it and you have restored that quality of life you can go home that day -"I've actually done something for that individual today." And you get a letter sent in to the Inspector or Sergeant saying, "I've had dealings with Jim Palmer and XYZ have been done and thank you very much" sort of thing. That's satisfaction. It's nice and it does make all the difference.

POST OFFICE – NOW

Amerjit Atwal (Amy)

Background

I was born in Nottingham, in 1959. My dad was a shop fitter in one of the factories at Melton Mowbray. My mother worked in a needle factory, a sewing factory. When she had the children she worked from home for Burton Group sewing, hand sewing sleeves into suits. In India, dad was a cook in the army.

(They) came over because they thought there was a better life in England. Mum still tells stories: she'd not seen snow and she remembers having to wear boots and it was just so cold. I think my mum was a bit spoilt because she'd come from a background where she hadn't had to work. They had servants in the house. She wasn't used to cleaning or cooking so that was a real shock for her. My dad really was quite spoilt because his parents came from an army background so they had servants. I think life was not what it seemed, when they came over. People think the grass is greener on the other side. It was a bit of cultural shock.

We lived in a large Victorian house near the Arboretum in Nottingham, 4 storeys high. No central heating. Most of the rooms had fires. I remember the coal men coming from the alley way at the back of the house. My dad had allotments in Mapperley, He had 2 massive greenhouses. He grew everything: gooseberry bushes, raspberry bushes, strawberries, sweet corn, peas, salad you name it. We were quite self-sufficient.

I remember the train station being built at Victoria Centre and going to Skegness from there. We used to go to Skegness on day trips from there - that's why I probably don't go to Skegness now.

School, work and marriage

I went to Glaisdale School and got my GCSEs. I went to Bilborough College and did English and Geography "A" levels. During my "A" levels, when I was about 18, unfortunately, it was quite tragic, my father died. I didn't go into further education, though I was thinking of going into something like teaching but with the situation at home… mum needed support, so, being the eldest, I got a job working in the head office at Boots in Beeston in the marketing department for about 4 or 5 years.

When I married, we moved to Leamington Spa where I worked for Powergen in the accounts department. (My husband, Lakbir, and I) met through a marriage bureau. It wasn't what you call traditional. We were introduced, he came over, we talked, spoke on the phone and we seemed to get on fine. We met a few times and within 6 months we got married - that's how it happened. (We are very happy in the marriage) but it wasn't what I call an arranged marriage. It's not like the old times. When my mum got married she saw my dad for the first time and that was it. I don't think they had much say in those days.

Moving to Chellaston Post office

I was going through a stage at work where it was privatised, as all the utilities were, and I said, "Right I just don't want to work in an office". We'd looked at various businesses and I wasn't too impressed. I said, "Well I want something a bit more stimulating than just sitting in a fruit and veg shop". The Post Office seemed like you're working with the general public, you're also having to use a bit of initiative, use your mind rather than just serving customers. So we looked around. We looked in (the) East Midlands and Chellaston was the second one we'd seen. There were lots of factors which really swayed us. Some were small and very rural and I'm thinking "Are you going to get the business there?" This was on a main road, quite a thriving place. The previous owners, Valerie and Mick, wanted to move to Cornwall.

(To buy a Post Office) you go through the estate agents, as you would a normal business. We were the only ones, I think, who had put something through, so there wasn't any competition as such, but I should think now things have changed. You have to put a business plan, obviously, it's to do with sales and everything; it's a bit more involved now.

(The Post Office) would give you a core payment, determined by how many people are going through. There's the set payments, the Post Office pay you and then anything additional, other transactions are incorporated in it. Unfortunately, over the years there's been a real downturn, which is a bit worrying.

I came in before computers came in; everything was manual. So like car tax, you would have to write it down on a form. You'd have to transpose it to another form to send off. I would have to check all the paperwork before I sent it off, so you can imagine how laborious. Each car tax disc number had to be written - you can imagine how long that would take. In those days you were paid on the basis of how long each transaction would take. BT bills, you would have to write each one of them down on another sheet, transpose it on to another sheet etc - it's just so much paperwork, unbelievable, when I first started.

I'm not knocking the internet, but it has shortcomings, unfortunately, for the Post Office. My profits are dropping, because a lot of people can do most things online now: people can do car tax online, mailing online. You can do Premium Bonds online.

My car tax has more than halved. We used to have queues out the door from when it was the end of the month. I just don't get that now. NSI, we won't be able to do that now. Premium Bonds up to a point, but anything to do with National Savings, investments, they're taking off the Post Office. You can only do those online. So in that respect, yes, I am seeing a gradual downturn in the Post Office.

Training.

We were given 2 or 3 weeks training, which isn't much really, considering how many transactions there are in the Post Office. We had a trainer who trained both of us. My husband stayed at the premises (for the training period) but he had his job as well. He doesn't run the Post Office; he's got his own career (as a teacher).

I can remember on the first day (of training) that they were queuing near the chemist because, obviously, in those days everybody had books and it was all manual - very time-consuming and laborious. Some of the customers still say they can remember me - I was sort of like shell-shocked. You don't know what's hit you. I just couldn't get rid of the queue! I think that, obviously, customers were complaining but they had to understand we were learning at that time. There was just so much to take in.

We have to balance the office every Wednesday, that's when everything's counted in the office, your stock, your money, every single stamp. You can imagine what a big job it is. All the car tax had to balance and everything. So the first balance was fine - I had my trainer with me. (Without the trainer) on the second balance - not having a clue, really, what you're doing - I was still balancing at one in the morning, still counting things! Now, we've got it to a T; you do a lot of your balancing as the day goes on and then you can just press a button.

Running the post office

First thing in the morning the Post Office side is not open until 8-30 am, but I actually open the shop side at 6 o'clock for newspapers. I have a gentleman who sorts my papers out Monday to Friday and I sort them out Saturday to Sunday, so he starts his deliveries from 6 onwards and the boys come from 7 onwards, to do their deliveries before they go to school. I have to get everything ready by 8-30, put all the money out, all the stock out, all the stamps etc. out.

Monday is the busiest day. We get the pensioners come in thinking that the money's going to run out. When I first took over there wasn't any confectionary, so everybody used to stand outside the shop for 8-30 and that's when I initially opened, but now the shop side's open they can queue inside the Post Office, which can get a bit precarious because I get the children in from school.

What's happened over the years is that the government have not encouraged people to use the Post Office, so people are having their new pensions put straight into the bank. We don't get so many young mothers coming in to the Post Office now for the family allowance because everything's put into the bank; the queues are not what they were.

By the time I've closed up, tidied the papers up, stocked the shelves or whatever, you're talking about 7pm sometimes and then I've done reports and everything. I never think of how many hours I've worked. I'm used to it, I suppose. I have tried going to bed early but I'm still up at 4.30a.m. so I think I can survive on about 5 hours sleep.

I haven't had a holiday. ... I've got the newspapers, the Post Office. I've had Christmas days off. To get somebody to run it ... I wouldn't be able to enjoy my holiday. It doesn't bother me, really, because I'd be just thinking about the place, "Is it being run as it should be?"

Ebay

Last thing at night, at half 4, we seem to get inundated with e-bay customers. That is a godsend to the Post Office, because we lost so much other transactions. People are selling items over the internet on e-bay. A lot of customers, who have sold their goods just rush in last thing at night, get them dispatched.

A lot of people e-bay now, perhaps if they're moving house and getting rid of things, (or) are looking at things lying in the garage collecting dust - whereas people used to take them to charity shops etc. They think, "Right, that could go" and it's amazing, really, what does go. I'm not sure of the percentage (e-bay takes) but, by the time the customer's paid e-bay etc., you're talking about whatever they're making's quite minimal, really.

We've had all sorts of obscure items. One of the customers had sold his car over e-bay. Over a number of months or perhaps half a year he managed to dismantle the whole of his car and sold parts. He'd wrapped up bits, components - it took him, I don't know how long. Over the months he came in with pieces, don't know how he'd managed to wrap them up; we often used to think, "Well that's not going to make it" - there were bits hanging out of the wrapped up pieces, very strange.

I don't know what sort of car it was, whether it was a Mini or something. But the last resort was when he brought his engine and we asked him how much it weighed and he said, "Oh, it's not very much, only 10 kilos" and he left it on the floor. They came to pick it up and then returned it saying, "We can't take this, it's well over 30 kilos". Fortunately, I knew where he lived and was able to leave a card for him saying, "Can you come and pick this up?" We couldn't reimburse his money. But the way he said, "Oh no, it doesn't weigh much!" So now if it's over 10 kilos we can't actually take anything, we have to weigh everything. I don't take it on face value now.

A lot of clothing's going out; people have got businesses selling. One of the customers sells sewing sets; somebody else sells white paint brushes and things like that. Whether some people actually buy them in bulk and sell them. Beads, that's another one which is a good earner for one of the customers. She sells all sorts of beads abroad to make bracelets. She comes in most days. Model railways, that's a good one and a lot of people have saved magazines over the years, all sorts of magazines, to do with cars and railways, comics people have kept; they seem to be collectors' items now.

We've lost so much other business, it's a godsend to the Post Office. Had it not been for e-bay I think the Post Office would be in dire straits.

Changes in sending letters and cards

At one time or other somebody will have to send a letter, they are few and far between. It's the older generation who will send letters and buy books of stamps. The next generation will send e-mails. There's different ways of communicating now, rather than sending things through the post. Nobody sends post cards. At Christmas people send cards but even that is dwindling. There's less and less people sending things abroad now.

The Retail Side

When we first started, when we walked into the shop it was like a DIY shop, because everywhere in the shop there were screwdrivers hanging up, screws and everything. He was into DIY, the last person. Over the years, we've sort of developed the cards, stationery and confectionery, especially the cards - they're a good selection, actually, quite reasonable in comparison to what you would pay in the town.

I've cut down on the sweets. I don't keep as many as I used to. There is a problem, unfortunately, and I should think most shops find that they have a problem with school children. If you're not watching them, you get things disappearing off the shelf. In the afternoons I do have restrictions on how many children can come in or else if I'm not out there to supervise… I don't let the children come in when it's a busy time. They'll take things, not queue up, and just walk out and you're not aware that they're actually there.

A lot of stock used to just disappear - and that doesn't go just for children. I think one Christmas I'd got chocolate out there and suddenly it just disappeared. One of the customers had come to me and said, "Do you realise that man has just walked out with your Ferrero Rocher?"

Chellaston Post Office, Derby Rd

Postmistress, Amerjit (Amy) Atwal, in front of the Post Office counter

News agency

The Post Office was approached and took over the news agency business when the newsagents' on High St wanted to sell and convert to a betting shop.

We thought, "Well you're going to get an influx of more customers". They would use the Post Office; use the newsagents, they marry together really. We thought it was a good investment. So we took it on - obviously quite naïve - not knowing the pitfalls and what it actually entailed, working 7 days a week. Before (we had the news agency)the Post Office used to close at 1-30 on a Saturday and at least I would get Saturday and Sundays - another aspect which we hadn't really thought about.

Financially we're not sure: we're just about breaking even – it's just a service, we're providing to customers rather than it being a profit making venture.

There never has been any money in newsagents: by the time you've paid your outgoings to all the paper boys, your delivery to W H Smith and try and get people to come and pay their bills.

We send reminders out and I have had cases where I've actually been round to collect them and they've already left without paying the bills, (or) we've been round to customers and they've promised to send us a cheque, then I've left it a week or two and they've gone, so obviously they had no intention - that is the downfall of that side. But now I do try to keep on top of it. There are certain no-go areas I will not deliver to because they just don't pay their bills.

Delivery boys and girls

Before, you were talking about over 20 houses (per round). That's gone down since I first took them over – it's between 10 and 15 at the most now. They have very small rounds now; they're pretty quick - morning papers half an hour or so. They're on their bikes.

Now, a lot of people have got other ways of getting news. They will look on the internet, rather than read the papers, they'll listen to the news, and they've got i-phones. Probably the older generation still like to read the newspaper.

There's about 9 (delivery boys and girls) in the morning and then about 10 or 11 in the evening and then I have the Sunday ones. They're separate. There's about 6 or 7 on a Sunday. It's between £8 and £13. £8 for evening papers and between £10 and whatever- it depends on how many papers they deliver. I've got a really good set of boys and girls now; they're very reliable, unless they're sick or there's holidays they all turn up on time and I know if there's a problem they'll ring up.

Years ago a lot of them would leave at the age of 15 - they'd get a Saturday job or get a job elsewhere. I have so many people waiting but they just don't leave now - some of the boys would be with me from the age of 13 right up to when they go to university - whereas before I had such a high turnover they'd be able to get Saturday jobs or they'd do odd jobs. There's just nothing out there for them.

Customers

Some of the customers haven't got family - it's like a social element really. This is probably the first time they've spoken to somebody in a whole week so you do get to know the background and all their health, medical ailments etc. Some of them are completely on their own, very isolated. I think if they know that you're a good listener, (and) can give them a bit of advice, it does them a world of good. A lot of them have said they won't go to the bank because it's so impersonal. You're in and out; you're just a number, aren't you? Whereas, over the years, they've got to know all the staff and, any personal issues or if they've got problems, they know they can talk to me or any of the other staff and get some good advice.

I first started when (we had) the pension books and we had certain customers who were always losing their books and you used to have to say, "Right you're going to keep it in your teapot" or "You're going to keep it so and so" and we used to have to try and remind them where it was!

Humorous moments.

One of the customers - he's no longer with us now - he passed away quite a few years ago, but he was a jolly little fellow. He used to come in the Post Office and used to divulge all sorts of information on his medical problems. One day we asked how he was, we'd not seen him for a few weeks. He said he'd been in hospital and he'd had an operation done. We didn't ask him what the operation was but he continued to go into great detail of what his operation was and then, all of a sudden, in the Post Office he dropped his trousers. We said, "Can you put them back up Mr ..." but he wanted to show where his scar was. That was quite embarrassing, really, but he had no qualms. And he used to go and buy cards and we used to say, "Who's the card for?" he says, "I want a brother card," although he'd not got a brother. He was quite a comical character.

The staff

I've got 2 part-timers and a Saturday girl - a good set of staff - they're hard to come by. There's so much background knowledge you have to know. Both have worked within the Post Office previously, so they're all Post Office trained.

Pleasures of the job

(I enjoy) communicating with people, talking to them (if) they don't know what to do sending a parcel or they want to send some money abroad or about car tax. I had a lady, unfortunately, her husband's become incapable and she's had to come and tax the car. She didn't know what documents (she needed), so she brought them all to me and said, "I just don't know what to do. What am I doing?" We went through it in great detail and she was just so grateful because she'd never had to do this. Her husband did everything before. It just makes you think that you've achieved something - gives you great satisfaction.

The old Chellaston Post Office next to the old petrol station on Derby Rd. before the current one was built. The Chinese take-away is now on this site.

Old Co-op to the right, The New Inn (now the Corner Pin) on the left. The adjoining cottages are now demolished. The man with a coal cart was a porter at Chellaston Station.

Copeland's Wood Yard, Station Rd. c1900, Later became Crockers' Yard at the top of Station Rd.

Alf Copeland (above right) and workers. Unknown date.

MARQUEE HIRE – FROM THE 30s

Richard Crocker

The Crocker Family

(Grandfather) came originally from Somerset. He was a designer at the railway. His major invention was a braking system and also, a machine for putting on railway carriages to test the vibration. In the 20s or 30s it was revolutionary. He also had something to do with the toilets on the trains. That's always been a family joke.

He lived on Walbrook Road then he bought Pear Tree Cottage (where) he lived until his death and Henry took it over. My grandfather retired from the railway and set his three sons, Fred, Henry and Lawrence, up with a building and joinery firm roundabout 1932. My father was Frederick. Everything went all right until the war but then all the men were called up and left just the three brothers who were (in their) late thirties, and they only bitted and bobbed during the war.

After the war, Mr. Banks of Banks's Better Blinds, phoned my father and said, "Do your guys know how to put tents up?" (My father) said, "Well, we've seen the lads do it. We've helped them when it's windy but we don't really know." (Banks) obviously had the same problem. All his guys had been called up, and the story goes that he got about 20 blokes and he put the whole of Derby Show up in about 2 days. It was a bit trial and error - they put them up, they fell down, they put them up. After that, my father says he sent Banks a bill for £350 which seems a hell of a lot of money. Mr Banks said, "You bring me £50 instead and you can have all the bloody tents cos I don't want them anymore." And that was really how they got into marquees. At the same time they were running transport all year round. The marquee business was just Easter to September, doing the local flower shows. Shortly after the war, Lawrence went farming at Wilne and round about 1950 Henry and Fred split up mainly to transport. (In) the late '60s the transport was gradually phased out and it went purely to marquees and marquee manufacture.

Education, Queen Elizabeth's, Ashbourne

I was born and bred in Chellaston. My father (Fred) had always worked for Crocker Brothers. He was an apprentice bricklayer. I was born next door to here, 20 Station Road, 1945. My mother died when I was five. (Father) never really showed any feelings, a bit distant. My sister looked after me from 5 to 7 and then we had house-keepers. I went to Ashbourne Queen Elizabeth Boarding School at 11 and my father remarried and moved to Chaddesden. So eleven to sixteen, I was away at school.

Initially it was tough. In the old days there was a fair amount of bullying. Fortunately I was a pretty good footballer and pretty good rugby player so I got accepted more than some of the others. One of the things they used to do was with the big square laundry baskets, they used to put you in a laundry basket and slide you down the stairs. Bit by bit the bullying went out. Eventually I quite got to enjoy the boarding school.

Rolls Royce

I got an engineering apprenticeship with Rolls Royce. We moved around, 6 weeks here, 12 weeks there, maybe 6 months in the old Drawing Office Training School on Ascot Drive. You did your first year in the machine shop on Sandown Road, which is long since gone, then 6 months in the Drawing Office Training School.

The first job I had was 12 weeks at Mountsorrel then you'd move round the different departments, mainly within Nightingale Road. When I finished my apprenticeship I went to Planning Inventory and Production Control, which was the movement of materials, tools, drawings to make sure everything got to the right place at the right time. I was there for 14 or 15 years.

I got married when I was 22 and moved back to Station Rd. two doors away from where I was born.

Crockers' in the 70s

My father was in his 70s and the paperwork and everything was building up. I left Rolls Royce and started here I guess April '75. The theory was that I was going to take over a lot of the paperwork and organise it, cos the systems here were virtually non-existent. The paperwork was terrible. I tried to iron that out. I'd learnt a lot of logical procedures at Rolls Royce. They'd got much more structure, procedures and systems of work.

Everything was a bit haphazard. It didn't seem to be very well organised and that was the first thing I got stuck into. Just putting up notes on boards for where we were going and what we were doing. My father was still involved a little bit. Staff in winter was down to about 3 or 4 people, plus me, Geoff, Margaret Jordan who worked in the office in the caravan and 3 foremen, Alec Steward, Ken Howitt, Dave Beckworth.

Most of the stuff was Findern Fete and that sort of thing. Local garden parties, local shows. In those days weddings were nothing like as prevalent as they are now. I managed to get the contract for Derby Show. Bit by bit we started getting more of the further away shows: Moreton in the Marsh, then Westmorland, Liverpool, Hull.

Before, everything had to be lifted by hand, put on the lorries. Fork trucks (are used) now - onto pallets, onto the lorry. Obviously it was a very big macho thing, who could lift something. Health and Safety Executive would have a fit now if they saw someone trying to carry nine tables on his head at the same time, which was a bit of a dare, but that's the sort of thing. People were expected to start at 16 and be able to lift probably a 1 cwt. bag straight off the floor. Some of the staff we had could, but most people couldn't. Originally you had to sledge hammer all the steel pegs in; now it's a mechanical breaker. It's like a road drill that hammers pegs in - much, much easier.

Manufacturing

(Manufacturing) goes back to the days when my father bought the business off Banks's. Banks's made all the tents. They'd got all the patterns – templates - for everything and my father just learnt how to sew. He did most of the sewing in those days. So really we just carried on. If you got a piece of canvas from a Banks's tent from 1930 it would still fit what we've got today albeit totally different material. When I first started virtually everything we'd got was canvas and sewn. The good stuff was made with English cotton and the crap was Egyptian and Indian cotton which changed over time and got better. Waterproofing techniques weren't too bad when new but obviously with canvas the waterproofing would gradually fade. We used to rub beeswax on the thread to fill the holes round the thread although most of them leaked to a certain degree. There was a fireproofing technique as well (but) it could be washed out, leached out of the material.

Gradually we started getting pvc-coated nylon. Obviously the material was infinitely stronger than canvas and it didn't rot like canvas. You could really keep it quite wet and it wouldn't get mildew, but then we found out that the nylon would degrade inside the material with sunlight so this gradually went over to pvc-coated terylene which was much better. We had an electric arc welder, which fuses the bits together. So in theory you've now got a complete waterproof membrane for the roof and the walls of the tent. The pvc you could clean it. You could wash it down. You get fungus in the core even with the newer materials. The older materials were better but due to the wonderful EU Health and Safety regulations they're not allowed to put arsenic in the material anymore and arsenic was the one thing that kept the fungus down.

(Tents) were made in narrow strips then put all together mainly on the floor or on a huge workbench - quite often on the floor because it was so big. They're still cut out by hand because most of the stuff you do is a one off, it's not worth having machines to do it. We're not turning out thousands of the same thing so it's cut out by hand then welded upstairs into pieces. There's eyeleting machines now. You don't have to knock them all in by hand like you used to.

When I was quite small, the only sizes we had were twenty or thirty feet wide. That was the biggest we went. I can remember my father actually made a 100 x 40 foot. Now that was a huge tent. It was a big day out when we had to put a 100 x 40 up. Now it's, "A 100 x 40? Yeah, we can do that in the morning." Over the years we've gone from 40 foot wide to 50 foot wide then 80 foot wide. Now 100 foot wide is the maximum tent we've got. Up to 300, 320 x 100 feet is possible.

First computer

When I first started the system wasn't too bad. It was triplicate, a card at the back, a pink copy and a yellow copy, stored in date order of the job and it was written on who it was and what they wanted, 40, 30 chairs, 40 tables etc. (One) copy was the foreman's when he got to load. The only problem was that people would change things and there were so many crossings out that you hadn't got a clue what it was all about, so that was a problem.

Then, 80s, we were still in the caravan – didn't move into the office until 91 - we spent £12,000 on our first computer which was an absolute nightmare. It was a great big thing. You had to put the discs in and wait for it to warm up; you had to back it up every night with great discs. Everything had to be the right temperature; it had to be immaculately clean. One thing that did happen was a guy wrote all our programs which have gradually been rewritten and rewritten, so we're using our own programs which we spent all that money on all those years ago.

You can buy a good computer now for £400! Things have changed. Now everything's computerised: print off mailing lists, computerised copies going. We very rarely send a brochure out now. There's twice as much information on line.

Marquee crews in the past

There were some good lads, good workers, but there were some, not quite itinerants, worked here, there, worked everywhere, and with it being a physical job they got very strong which did tend to lead to fighting. Most of them had got prison records for one thing and another. Thieving scrap was their favourite game cos it was easy money.

All sorts of things have happened over the years. Most of the guys were heavy drinkers. They were very good at not drinking during the day but once they knocked off, that was it, they'd get wrecked. (One) time they were working at the North Wales Show at Caernarvon and somehow got into trouble in a pub. One of the lads decided to jump over a fence to get out of the way but he didn't realise there was a 30 foot drop on the other side. He went straight down and broke his leg.

Then, early one morning, going to go to Chatsworth Horse Trials, it was a bit damp, six or seven in the morning. I went down to the tents. Next thing Tony came up with a nice new pair of boots on. "Glad to see you've got some new boots, Tony." I thought back and I was sure I'd seen him early in the morning with his dirty old baseball boots on. Apparently somebody with a caravan had taken their nice new hiking boots off, put them under the caravan and obviously gone to bed. Tony had seen these early in the morning and some poor guy had got up to find a pair of smelly old baseball boots under the caravan.

These rough buggers, they've been on site, something's disappeared so they must've had it. Anything on a show ground is fair game. Not really stealing it but anything that's been left around like a stack of plywood or anything like that, they'd come back with it loaded and head for the hills.

Crockers' lorry in the 50s. Richard Crocker is the boy 2nd from left on top of the lorry

Two workers at Crockers' in the 1940s. Heinz, a German Prisoner of War on left

Henry Crocker at work in the 40s

Crockers' workers in the 40s

We did a job at Alton Towers sponsored by Cadbury's Wispa bar. I must have been away somewhere. When they went on the Sunday morning to take this quite small tent down apparently there was a thick end of 2 ton of Wispa bars waiting to be chucked away. They must have been left out all night in the boxes. So they put all this on the pick-up then found they couldn't get the tent on the pickup. So they came back to Derby with the 2 ton of Wispa bars, which broke the back axle on the pick-up, sold the lot for quite a lot of money and then had to go back and fetch the tent down.

Originally we used to have what we called the Kip Tent. As soon as you got on site you put your own tent up and you camped at the tent on site. They all went out one night in Liverpool, left the Kip Tent; someone went into the Kip Tent, chucked petrol on it and burnt the lot down. After the fire that was the end of the Kip Tent. We moved on to caravans. We still use caravans now, but a lot of digs - all round the country; the main ones are at RAF Waddington. It's easier once they're on site if they live in caravans - hotel bills would be heavy with the security and the distance.

Type of venues now

We're moving more into shows; doing a lot more work locally because of the cost of transport; it's a sign of the times. People are cutting back so we're having to take on smaller work, keep less men on the sheet. I think it's going to be quite a poor year for us. We seem to go in 10 year cycles. We had the recession in '91 which was tough. Then in 2001 we'd got Foot and Mouth; most agricultural shows were cancelled, which knocked our turnover by about nearly £200,000 a year. When I first started, the turnover was something like £50,000; now I'd say it's pushing £900,000 - down a little bit, but it has been up to a million. Before, in the winter, it was, "Sorry can't be bothered." But things have changed. We have a famous saying – "Now is the winter of our discount tents!"

The smallest tent we've got now is 3 metres square. £95 plus VAT, if you wanted to hire it in Derbyshire, next week for the weekend. For a wedding, all season, absolute minimum, with the basics, £20 pounds a head. With a bit more refinement, £30 pounds a head and then you could be up to £40 pounds a head for absolutely top of the range with generators, mobile toilets and all that.

We did a 40th birthday party last week where our bill was about £24,000 – £25,000 for which we did no electrics, no lighting, no dance floors and a minimum amount of furniture which was all done by somebody else. For the party itself you can double that - something around £50,000 - before the fireworks, and anything to eat and drink. The number of guests was 80, so this party must have cost at least £100,000!

(Our marquee at Derbyshire cricket ground) - that's permanent. It's 39 x15 metres. We made it for them, delivered it for them. It's not just for hospitality at the cricket; it might be booked out tonight for a party, this afternoon for a wedding. Anything really, they use it all the time. That was a sale job. I think it was £230,000, there might have been additions, but I'm not saying I made a vast amount of profit out of it.

Weddings

Years ago we often used to get weddings for 300 or 400 (people). Now a big wedding is 120, loads of 80s, 70s, 100s, occasionally 150. It's the cost of it all: £2,000 to £3,000 for a wedding, that's about the average. At one time we took a decision to take no wedding work from the middle of June till the beginning of September. (Now) you need your weddings when other jobs have dried up. They're an absolute pain. Have you running backwards and forwards. "I didn't expect the pink to be that shade of pink." "It's bigger than I'd thought it would be," "I wanted another 6 inches." "I've got a wonky table." "Can I have a extra table?" This isn't right; that isn't right. It really is a nightmare. Do you go to a hotel and ask them to change the wallpaper or change the chairs? They're looking at different chairs; they're changing the colour of chairs, "Oh, I don't want white now, I want silver. I don't want silver, I want gold. If I have gold, I'll have pink pads." Every day they're phoning for something else.

They look like a battle ground when you go in afterwards. If people dropped a pat of butter at home they'd pick it up and clean the carpet but they just leave it and it all gets trodden in to a horrible greasy mess. One of our biggest bugbears is getting rid of carpets. It costs us £100 or something to hire a skip so we're stuck with carpet we don't want. (If) I could find somebody who could be bothered to cut bits out of it, they can have it. We've got tons of it. This week we'll get through perhaps twenty 50 metre rolls of carpet we've got to get rid of. We're not allowed to burn it so it's all got to go in the skip.

Problems with marquees

We used to do caravan exhibitions every winter. About late 70s, early 80s, we had one for Don Amott - 2 thundering great big tents up there. Horrendous winds, the lot - 65 to 70 caravans inside were virtually wrecked. The tents were all over the yard and we reckoned that it cost us about £13.000 which in the late 70s was a good lump of cash.

The last one I remember going down was 10 years ago at Peterborough in a huge wind. I'm damn sure it wasn't our fault. We were fined by the Health and Safety Executive for not giving sufficient indication to the people inside when they should evacuate the tent. Well, how hot do you have to be before you decide you're on fire? Bit of common sense but we got a fairly stinging fine. We don't get so many disasters as such now.

There are some strange rules on tents. 20 years ago you just made a tent and shoved it up and if it fell down, tough. Now, any new design, any new size over 40 feet you've got to have wind calculations tested, which is really a bit of a nonsense because it depends on how well it's been put up and how tight someone's pulled the ropes. If something's been put up properly, it should stand whatever wind speed. The tents are still pretty similar to what the Bedouin have been using for thousands of years. You get to know some days it's too windy to get them up.

One of our best cock-ups ever (was) with a guy who wanted a 60 x 40 lambing tent at Lichfield. We quoted him a price. I didn't know there were two Lichfields and the other one's just the bottom side of the M4 which is where it was. So we had to trail all the way down to Hampshire, I think it was, with this 60 x 40 lambing tent. But you live and learn. It makes you think twice - always to question an address (in case there's) more than one.

Thirty years ago there was very little vandalism. You could put a tent up and leave it. Then all of a sudden, 20 years ago they started getting slashed and cut up and written all over. Now we don't get anything like as much, possibly because we're a lot more careful. You do occasionally get a few knife slashes but not very much. They tend to slash the tent to see what's inside. That's it, if there's nothing inside they're not bothered.

Graffiti is more of a problem - some of it intentional; people just write on the wall, " Ice Creams £1," or something like that in marker pen. A permanent marker will stain the material. That can be an absolute pain. We've had some drawings people have done. The famous one is two pigs fornicating which almost ended up at a wedding job. We just had to take that section out. More often than not it's just idiotic scribble.

Once we leave site the customer's responsible till we come back, so it's up to them otherwise they get hit with a thundering great bill.

In the wash

(Cleaning tents) was always one of my bugbears. It was a lousy job. Everybody hated it. You had a big concrete pad about 50 foot square and we used electric floor scrubbers and detergent. Electricity and water aren't a good idea to start off with. You've got the tent to clean but you couldn't really rinse them off properly, couldn't dry them properly. It got rid of lots of the muck but it never got them properly clean. A guy at Uttoxeter he'd got a washing machine. We took stuff over there and started using his.

It must have been about 2003 we bought a Spanish machine. It was 120,000 Euros I think. We had to take the floor out of the upstairs workshops so we could get the damn thing in. It stands about 6 metres high, 6 and a half metres wide and about 4 metres to the end. There's a drier in the washing machine. (The tent) goes through like a vertical car wash with 2 big brushes and as it comes out there's some squeegees press on to it, 2 big fans blow on it then it's wound between a series of hot rollers. They dry the plastic out but they don't dry the edges. They need a bit of a wipe but they're virtually dry. We've had it 7 or 8 years now and it gets used (mostly) in the winter cos we wash everything - our washing is a bit like the Forth Bridge, it never all gets done. If we didn't do other people's we might get all our own done but then in the winter you need to earn a crust and it's taken about £15 - £20,000 this winter.

Richard Crocker by the drying machine

Richard Crocker and lorry

Workforce now

Our main season doesn't really start till round about Easter. We don't really start getting pulled out 'til the middle of June. Then from the middle of June to the middle of September you could be rushing about all weekend. We've got less men this year: somewhere between 15 and 20 cos some only come for a few days - some students.

Permanently in the office we've got 2 girls who do the accounts and the bookings, myself and Victoria who mainly do all the site visits and the measuring and quotations, Ian who looks after the manufacture side and works with me sorting out who does what. To a certain extent, Victoria's a hell of a lot better than me with colours and getting on with some of the women.

In the winter, in the manufacture (and) the office there'll be about 16 (in total), 6 in the office, (and) say 7 lads out there.

Six years ago we were gradually getting more and more problems getting English lads to work. They wanted £400 in their pocket and they're (only) happy working 9 to 5, 5 days a week. Certainly didn't want to work the weekend. In the morning we might expect 20 blokes to come in. Well, if you ever got anything like 18 you'd done well. More like 14, 15 turning in. It was getting a bigger and bigger problem. Some of them you got anyway were absolutely unemployable. No work ethic at all.

We got an email from Latvia. Do we want to employ Latvian workers? Through this agency the first year we had 6. They wanted to work every hour God sends. They'd work all weekend. Now we've had the same 6 back. One of them has done 6 years, 2 of them have done 5 years, the minimum is 2 years, good as gold and we just take one or two lads locally now. We bought a house for them cos we weren't sure where we were going to put them up, They're a hundred yards from their work.

These Latvians are probably going to be on, top line, something in the order of £500 a week. A good wage in Latvia is £200 a month so they're like millionaires when they go back. One's doing his house up. Some do a bit of work. They're paid the minimum wage here which is about £6 an hour plus overtime, plus if they're working away they get 'night out' money so they do an average week probably more than 40 hours, more like 60, 70 possibly. There's a lot of travelling as well, you see. Like this morning, 7 o'clock this morning they went to RAF Waddington. They'll do 12 hours today, which in pay terms is 18 hours. Tomorrow there's a gang going to the Bank of England in the morning Sunday, double time. And they've got to go to Maurice Lee (Memorial Park) at 5 o'clock so pay-wise they'll certainly be doing 70 hours.

Future prospects

Technically there will not be a Crocker when I've gone or retired. Geoff is my step-brother and Victoria's his daughter so I suppose there's a loose connection. He's looking to bring it on. Hopefully they will take it on and keep it going. One of my sons was involved but then he decided that he didn't really like it. He didn't want all the hours and he was better at computers anyway. The other one's never been involved.

MARQUEE HIRE - NOW

Bob Bradbury, Foreman at Crockers'

Childhood in Chellaston

I was born in '56 at 65, Ridgeway, (Chellaston). My father was a labourer on a building site and mother stayed at home. I've got six brothers and three sisters, so she didn't have time to go to work!

I quite often went down the brickyard; we used to climb down and across the steep quarries – like you've seen these rock climbers, going across with bare hands. We used to have a rope swing that used to swing right over the top of the quarry, which Graham Dalton fell off and broke both of his arms. But when you're a kid you don't see danger. If it had been raining, you'd get all the little streams coming down what had worked little valleys out and we used to build dams.

One time I was there – me and Alan Brailsford - and we actually got stuck in the clay. We was up to us knees in this soft clay, and it was a bit frightening, but then Stan Eley, who was the night watchman there on weekend shift - he had to come up and literally pull us out of this clay. He did tell us off but I was more frightened that he was going to nip home and tell me mam when he got back home.

Chellaston Brickyard

I didn't like school. I didn't have any formal qualifications. It was straight into labouring jobs. Me dad got me my first job, at Chellaston Brickyard, aged 15, in 1972. It was hard work – and hot – it was kilns for baking bricks and sheds for drying them and you was labouring in that heat - quite a hot, sweaty job.

There was three in the kilns, stacking bricks in kilns to be baked, two fetching them out of the kilns, ready baked, and on to the lorries, two lorry drivers, the actual gaffer, Fred Smithurst, a foreman, Ray Fogg. Four of us wheeled wet bricks into the drying shed. Jack Collins (was) up in the pan house where all the clay got crushed and pushed out of the machine. Then there was a digger driver at the bottom of the clay hole, loading the tub up and one lad who swapped hooks over on the tub and sorted the gypsum out from the clay.

(The gypsum) used to go to the plaster place up near Gotham. It's crushed and made into plaster. But quite often they used to bring pieces back which had been carved or shaped – they'd make eggs or ashtrays, things like that. And they'd bring them back and they'd be offered to the chaps at a cheap price.

The majority of the workforce came from Heanor and Eastwood. The foreman came from there. Jack Collins came from Melbourne. Several of us lived in Chellaston: Stan Eley, who lives in Chellaston was a larger than life character, a really pleasant chap, and Jake Osborne, who thought himself a bit of a Frank Sinatra - he'd often just be singing to a milk bottle! Made it a pleasant job, really.

They first start you off just fetching the dry bricks out, loading them onto a barrow - 50 bricks at a time - wheeling them to the kilns. There's another chap in there, he takes the bricks off the barrow and stacks them in the kiln drift for firing. Then you take the empty barrow back and fetch another load.

In the drying sheds and kilns

After you'd been there a short while, you'd get to work on the machine barrows. The wet clay was coming out of the press, through wires to cut it into the brick shapes. That was pushed onto a flat barrow and you used to take them from the machine into the drying shed and stack them up on the floor which was gas heated. When I was a young lad, they used to use coal fires to warm the floors up. I can remember going to the brickyard, fetching slack; we used to go and help ourselves to a little bit now and then, cus it was quite expensive stuff, in them days.

It was hard: it was hot - hot was the worst thing. You've got a shed with no walls on it, similar to a barn – and you'd stack the bricks up to fill the walls in. Then in the summer if you got a really hot day you'd take the walls down so you'd got a bit of air coming through. You were walking on hot floors so your feet was hot all the time – not as warm as in the kilns, though.

The two lads that fetched them out of the kilns, they had a bit of a hotter job – they loaded the bricks what had been baked, onto the conveyor belt (and) put them onto the lorry. The kilns had probably been switched off for a couple of days, (but) the bricks are still hot while you're in there fetchin' them out.

There was always three firemen and they used to have to stay there overnight, just keep their eyes on (things), switch the fires off at the right times, which was old Stan Eley, Stan's dad. Then there was Stan on it and I think another chap called Albert.

The three chaps in the kilns when I first came was Ernie Green, Jake Osborne and Lindo – never knew his second name. A lot of people who did start the job'd gone within a couple of weeks. They just didn't like the job, couldn't stand the heat. It wasn't a pleasant job to some people. Those three was there all the time I was, and they'd been there three years before.

Picking up hot bricks, you take the skin off your thumbs and your fingers. You used to get like a rubber pad made out of old inner tubes. You'd just cut two slices for your index finger and two slices for your little finger and then a little thumb pad, which you'd make yourself out of a little piece of rubber tube. And that was the specialised clothing what you got! They used to offer you a pair of boots at Christmas if you wanted 'em, but most people went for the turkey.

We didn't make facing bricks. They was just (for) internal walls or the bricks that you see if you open a man-hole up; it wasn't a quality brick – I suppose they was cheap and cheerful. Sometimes they'd have little cracks in 'em and they'd still throw 'em on the lorry rather than chucking them away.

They used to have what they called a brick stock – any bricks that weren't sold this week, they'd be stacked into a pile. It just seemed to get to the point at the end that the stock–pile was just getting larger and larger. It was run by Frank Sissons - must have been 1975/76 – and we was told that he was going to sell it up – he wasn't making profits. There's clay still there.

Chellaston Brickyard 1965

Crockers' Marquee Hire

Bob started work at Crockers' in 1976, aged 20. He has worked there since then and is now one of the foremen, working all year round.

There were no frame tents when I first started. Then they decided to try the aluminium structures. They've gone bigger and bigger – they now do one twenty metres wide which can stand an 80mph wind force. It's a lot better and a lot safer than what it was in the early times. The canvas (now is a) quite heavy duty industrial plastic. The sewing shed is a lot larger. They manufacture standard (and) a lot of bespoke tents. (Someone) will come in and say, "I need a tent that'll fit on the side of me lorry" - so then it's make it to measure so it fits on the lorry; adapt the lorry so it can carry the marquee. Most of the cutting's done by scissors. I don't have a lot to do with manufacturing.

I have a gang – normally there's 4 of us. You try and load your lorry in the night-time ready for in the morning. If you've got a bit of distance to travel – 50/60 mile- you'd be in at 7 o'clock.

We have a checklist, but you still do forget things. Hopefully there's someone in the yard, that can pop out, and bring whatever it is you've forgot. I went to a job at Alton Towers, walked round the lorry and thought, "Ayup, no steel pegs on!" I'm probably 150 steel pegs short and they're the first thing you need on the job so somebody's got to come up to you and you've just got to sit and wait for them to get there.

Our Workforce

I'm on salary - most of the foremen are on salary. The rest of the chaps (seasonal workers) are all paid hourly. There's 8 Russians or Latvians. They're all right. They're quite decent lads. Most of them are hard working. They've said in the past, an average working month for them is about £200- £250 in Latvia; they come over here, and they're earning that in a week - that plus. They send all the money back to Latvia. When they go back in September, they must have quite a large bank balance to last them the winter till they're ready to come back again in the May.

When I first started we was working 7 days a week and you could put 10 or 15 hours in every day. I got used to putting a lot of hours in. Nowadays they don't seem to want to do that. English people, quite often only want to work an 8 hour day. They don't want to work weekends. Whereas the Latvians come over, the wives or the families are in Latvia, so they're here solely to work. If you told them to work 20 hours a day and have 4 hours sleep, they'd be quite happy at that – just to be here working.

They're not the type that want to go out drinking so it doesn't matter whether it's Friday at 7 o'clock at night or what, whereas your English, come 6 o'clock, 7 o'clock, they're there - "Come on, we're going home, it's Friday night." It's good to have them coming over to do it, but then again, I sometimes think it's robbing English people o' jobs. If it was left to me and you could get the English to do it, I'd say yes, let English people, or British.

Putting up the marquees

Putting up Crockers' first frame tent at Alton Towers in the 1980s

On a 160 by 100 you've got 8 sections down each side - 16 sections. You want 4 men to pick each one of those 16 sections up comfortably; then you've got 6 king poles, 12 queen poles, then 6/700 steel pegs to hold that one up (and) all the walling which goes round it. At a guess, to weigh it, would be probably 4 or 5 tonnes. (They're worth) literally thousands, probably £30/40,000.

To put (a) 9 metres by 12 metres tent up, peg it down, and put the board flooring down inside it would probably (take) around 2 to 2 ½ hours for four chaps. With no flooring or anything in it, I would say an hour, an hour and a half.

A 160 by 40 - we put that one up at Trent College - takes a day's work, say 9 hours for 4, 5 or probably 6 men. It's not so much the tent itself - you want 1,000 pieces of flooring to put a board floor into it. Then they have a bar tent, changing rooms, a little kitchen on the back. To put the lining inside of it can take the best part of a day. Then awnings, walkways things like that, it all adds up. Trent College I'm there 4 days with probably 6 men doing that job.

If it's a frame, we build the top of it up on the floor, similar how you would a camping tent; then put the canvas on the top, then stand it up. Rain doesn't really matter - you get wet, you dry out. If it's windy that is one of the worst things. As soon as you've stood your legs up, you've suddenly made a sail! The wind hits it and it tries taking it away. If you try to hold the tent down, even a small tent, and it's blowing quite heavy, then you've got a job on to hold it and make it stay there.

So what we normally do is, we'll put it up without the tops in and then pull the tops in afterwards, when we can secure the legs of the frame. Other than that it's sort of wrestle with the wind – if it's not too bad a wind you can hang on and get a couple of pegs knocked in quickly just to make sure it stays there. But it can be a bit hair-raising. We have had one or two flip over and go rolling down the fields.

They will survive strong winds. If it's cold and it snows it'll stick to the top and slowly just push the top down, whereas water will just run off it. When the snow sticks to it, it just weighs down and starts making it sag, so if you don't get the snow off, eventually when it melts you've just got gallons and gallons of water on the top of the tent. So it can cause a lot of problems. They are pretty much 99% waterproof, most of them.

Wet ground for putting pegs in isn't ideal. The pegs are about two foot six long, so usually they get below the little soggy bit at the top and get in some firmer ground underneath, but the walling pegs around the outside of the walling, are only twelve inches long, so sometimes they'll pull out. That means extra work knocking pegs back in. We've got Cobras, which are like a pneumatic drill. They are hammers - we use them for knocking the pegs in – sledgehammer days have gone.

(The ropes) are polypropylene. They used to buy some ropes off the old aircraft carriers. There was two wires and ropes in between them to form a net across the boat - when the aircraft came in that was what it hooked itself onto to stop it. After so long they couldn't use them anymore, they'd worn too much to hold the plane back, so they used to sell those off and Crockers' used to buy those. They was extremely good ropes – never any problems with them snapping.

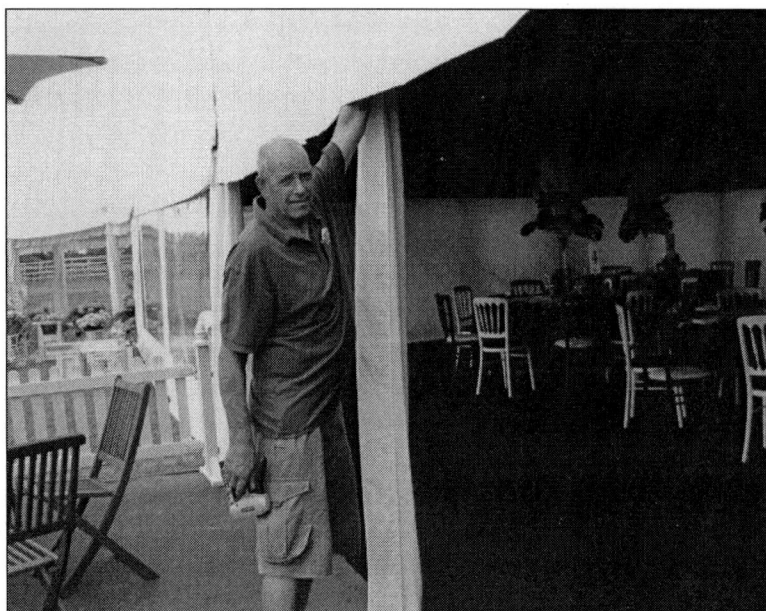

Bob putting up a marquee in 2011 for a client's 50th birthday

Distances travelled/venues

One of my furthest is Norfolk – Walsingham. Other than that it's Watford, Denbigh in Wales. I'm usually local; I do the jobs that are round about here – mainly wedding work, parties. I try and get a gang with me who don't want to eat café food, so I'll just drive straight to the job, and have a sandwich.

A lot of them go out and stay on the job: like the Denbigh Show; one of the other foremen goes up there for a week, staying in digs for the period he's putting the tents up and taking them down. We've had gangs in Ireland, Scotland. The Isle of Dogs is one of the furthest places I've been myself, the other side of London.

In the marquee hire side, we put that little bit more effort in. There's a lot of companies. We've just done a job for JCB – it involved putting nice, decent, clean tents up in a quarry. Because it's JCB, they want the best, so it's virtually new canvas, with a risk of it being damaged. They just go that little bit further to make the job right for them. A lot of companies wouldn't even quote for jobs like that.

I went and did a job for Joe Brown, the singer, a few years ago. (Then) Danny La Rue - very nice man. We went to his restaurant - it was like a stay-over place. He said "Just go in and get whatever you want to eat," and when we went in and looked at the menu it's chips, "Rolling Stones", "Mick Jagger" (would probably be a burger) - all these different famous names for each different type of food.

One of my favourites is Hari Krishna in Watford, the house that George Harrison left to them. It's a stately home and what they call their temple. (We go there) for like an open day, for people to go and visit the temple. At one time they was Crockers' biggest paying customer. We're there about a week - usually get digs nearby.

They've got a big cattle sanctuary, a really elaborate wooden shed for cows. They must have spent £5/600,000 on the shed and grounds. They are really friendly people; so it's a nice place to work. (A lot of them wear gowns) a yellowy cream one or some of them have orange; they all have strange names and their little spot and ponytail.

One tent was a donations tent. (Once) Richard went and they were counting all their money on the floor, literally thousands and thousands in donations. The main tent had a stage in it; they do a play, explaining to people how Hari Krishna started in England and how they all came over from India, bought the cows and made them sacred and told everyone not to eat meat any more. They've told us you must stay away from the Macdonald's down the road!

Usually at Universities it's for their graduation day. The Trent College one is up for about a week. They have a speech day, a summer ball and graduation day. We do Derby University graduation ball. Their party goes on through the night and then they have breakfast in the morning. Quite often if we go and fetch it in on a Saturday morning, they're walking down Ashbourne Rd coming away from the party just as we're arriving to take the tent down. Usually it's just a mass of burgers, squashed food, sick and whatever else on the floor – masses of it! They do move in and start cleaning it up, but we still see quite a lot of it. The worst thing on the linings is wine – especially if it's red wine – it takes quite a lot of getting out. Quite often if they are sick, they usually go outside and do it up the back of the tent, so you just have to watch it when you're pulling walling pegs out! It can be nasty!

I prefer to do wedding jobs, even though Crockers' is shying away from them. The big banqueting suites now, are offering such a good deal, cus they're bringing their prices down. People are saying, "What's the point of having a marquee? We can go there. There's no worries about the weather, it don't matter if it rains, shines, blows or whatever. Everything's there - they lay everything on.

It takes a lot to keep a bride happy. You could have just pulled the lining up and it's just hanging there, and you haven't tightened it back and they'll walk in - usually the bride, although the groom sometimes does cause some hassle - "Oh I don't like this. I don't like that... no, that's not right!" After all it's supposed to be their one and only time. And you think, "Well, let's finish it and then see if it's all right!" I'll spend a lot of time standing talking to 'em saying, "Well, yes, we can do that and the other," and I'm not really working - it's putting a lot of time on the jobs. But to me the wedding jobs are more enjoyable. I enjoy the challenge of a wedding, or a challenge of an awkward tent, something that don't quite fit and you've got to sort of make it fit – that's what I like. With agricultural shows, it's just a tent and a bit of furniture.

It's very rarely we go and put any up at Christmas. New Year's party – you're lucky if you do three now, whereas at one time you used to be working a couple of weeks before Christmas.

Toilet facilities/ graffiti

If we did use the toilet tents now, I think we'd have the environmental health round! It was a long ditch with a screen round it - the old urinals. On agricultural shows they used to do ones 12 foot square with partitions in and then a bucket in it - a proper tin toilet, like — ladies' and gents' as well. They were worse; when you took 'em down, the ladies' side was always in a worse state than the gents! It was terrible – some of them hadn't even done it in the bucket, they'd done it on the floor at the side. It was bad to take down! Maybe they was just saying something like, "Don't bring these again". At least with the urinals you just took the walling away and folded it up. Thankfully we don't do them anymore. We now have mobile toilets.

(Graffiti) is annoying because felt tip just don't come off the plastic. Quite often we have to chuck it away or cut the piece out and re-sew it together. We went to one job and they'd written on, "The best Crockers' sieve I've ever been in!" It was a long time ago and the tent leaked a bit. It's usually just a felt tip and a little bit of writing. You can't repeat what most of 'em write. Quite often it's the area where you are - like "The Red Army" or whatever football team it is nearby.

Cleaning the tents

We have Indian ink remover and that won't fetch felt tip off. There must be some sort of pores in the plastic - you'll fetch the main black of it off, but there'll be a grey outline still. The worst one I can remember they'd actually gone up on the top of the tent and done felt tip all over the top. It was even worse because the people who fetched it down and folded it up didn't say anything about it, so nobody knew about it until it went out the next time. It was quite offensive language.

(Tents) have an annual wash every winter, to be put away for the winter. Through the season, if it's raining they probably get washed every time they go out because if it's raining you're dropping it down onto sludge.

(The) big washing machine at work uses an industrial detergent. There's some wax what they have to use as well. The smell of curry stays on the tents for weeks, even when it's been washed. We have had times when (people have) done a barbecue inside the tent, then you can smell the barbecue on it all the time and that's as bad as the curry.

Other marquee companies bring their marquees and have them washed at Crockers'. We have a lot of the groundsheets out of the Army tents what they wash, so we must be getting quite a lot off the Ministry of Defence.

New tents or middles are what you use for the best jobs - a wedding job, a party or even universities, graduation dos. Then as they get older you use them for other jobs. 7-8 years old, it starts looking a bit bedraggled; it's still useful to go to a pub or to the carnival or things like that. As it gets a bit older still, say 15 – 20 years old it can then be used for cattle tents at shows.

Whoops!

I can't think of a disaster for me. I can remember one I wasn't actually involved in. It was Dave Beckworth, who used to work for us. They got the address and it was at a vicarage. So anyway, they pulls up at this job and there's no-one in the house, so they thought, "Well, the tent can only go there. It can't fit anywhere else." So they put the marquee up. Nobody turned up. Jumped in the wagon. Went back home. Crocker's got a phone call, "I live at such a place and somebody's gone and put one of your tents up in my back garden." They knew nothing about it; it should have been up the road, a couple of houses further up!

We had one phone up, going back a few years. The chap says, "Er, is there any chance you can come and take this tent down, only I want to cut me grass. It's about 2 foot long inside the tent now!" They'd forgot all about the tent! It was only a 30 foot square. They'd missed it, they knew they was short of a 30 foot square and didn't know where it was! It had been put up at this party and no-one had been and fetched it down again. If it was me, I'd have took it down myself and kept it.

Why I like the job

I like both sides of it – putting tents up and being in the yard, manufacturing. I can go into the shed to do a bit of welding, repairing. For the last three weeks I've been repairing flooring. Just levering bearers off a piece of floor and nailing a new piece on. I'm quite happy doing that. A lot of people would find that a bit boring, but I find if I'm doing something the time just flies by. I enjoy that type o' work. It's so satisfying.

Ferreting Hobby

I've got 26 ferrets, well the wife's got 26 ferrets or 22 I've got for the working ones. They are worth about £3-£4. We (used to) do a lot of showing with ferrets. I did breed a really dark strain and the most I've been offered for one was £300.

We always had ferrets when we was kids. Me Dad had ferrets. When I was about 7 or 8, I used to go out ferreting with Dad. Ken Smith from the end of St.Peter's Rd would often come round; he'd borrow me Dad's ferrets and nets and take me along catching rabbits. We'd go to Weston, the prisoner of war camp and places like that and we'd probably come back with three or four rabbits. Them days we used to eat the rabbits that we caught. One'd be for the table and the other three for sale. Very rare we eat 'em now. Now it's more a pest control and food for the ferrets.

In Chellaston there used to be a few rabbits up Sandy Hollow, at the top of Silverwood's farm – where the reeds on the old wetland is. I think they're still there now. There used to be some on Pit Close at the bottom of what they used to call the Ant Hill, the old quarry. A lot of people do go ferreting in Chellaston. A lot of my cousins and nephews still live here and most of them have got ferrets and nets. You can clear a warren out today and then next week you'll probably get a couple of rabbits in there again. They do move about.

You've got a warren which is probably, six holes, like a labyrinth underground. Some of those holes may be dead ends; some of them may lead to the exits that we can see. The theory is that ferret chases the rabbit out of one o' the exits. We put the net on each of the holes, drop the ferret in. The rabbit fears for its life when it gets the smell or sight of the ferret 'n decides to make an exit. It goes into the purse-net and then we catch the rabbit, kill it and the ferret goes back down to see if there's any more rabbits. Hopefully you just clear a warren like that.

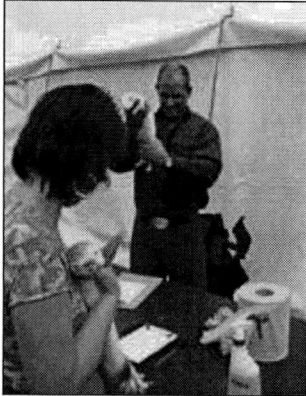

On an odd occasion it'll make a mistake and go to a dead end, in which case the ferret will try and climb over the top of the rabbit, trying to get to its head because they can kill them from the head end. If it can't get over it, it'll just sit at the back of the rabbit and scratch it. This could take minutes or even hours. Nowadays we use locators; the ferret's got a transmitter collar on it; we can pick up and find out where the ferret is. If it's been in one place for several minutes, we'll just dig down to the rabbit.

(People) phone me and ask me if I'll go and clear rabbits out for them. It is a free service; whatever rabbits we catch, we keep - that's the only payment we get. It may sound cruel, but we enjoy doing it. It is a pest control, but it's also a challenge – hunter gatherer type! It's usually for farmers. We do quite a lot in Staffordshire. You go to one farm doing a bit of ferretting and they'll tell the neighbouring farmer, then they want you to go onto their land.

We was spending every weekend in Staffordshire, but we've just been recently asked if we'll go and do a churchyard at Wychnor just outside Burton. They're borrowing underneath the graves and the headstones are tilting, or lowering theselves into the borrows. I says, "I'll do it, but I want written permission, because if I'm there with a spade in a graveyard, the police are forced to come out and see me. They'll want to know what I'm doing, so I need it written down that I'm there on a pest control!"

HAIRDRESSER – THEN and NOW

Mary Christie

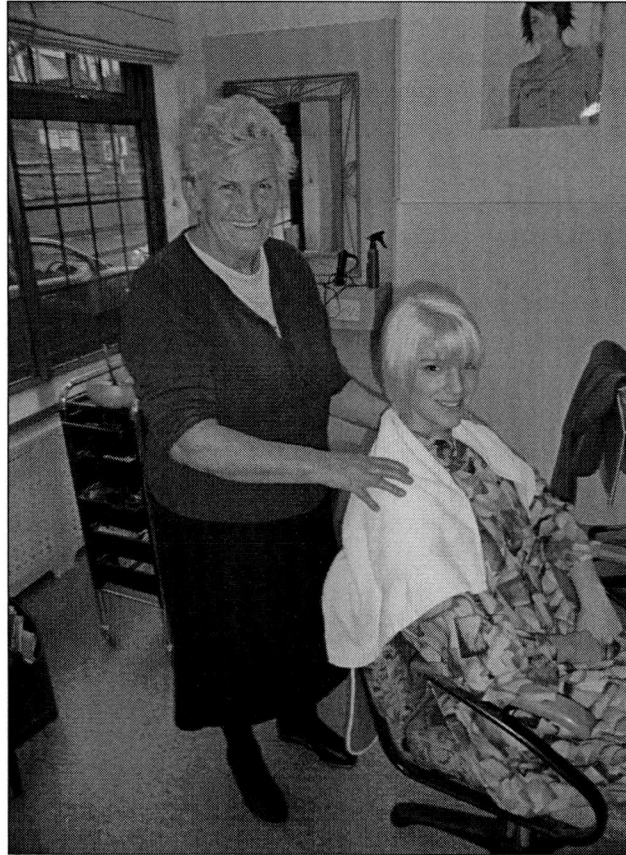

Mary at work in 2011 at Christie's, 32 High St.

Early days

As far as I know, I was born down by Bold Lane. My father got killed on Uttoxeter Old Rd, going to Mass. (That) left me and Mum on our own. So we lived (as lodgers) in rooms down the West End – only one room. Eventually we got two. Mum went cleaning, scrubbing, and then she had to go on munitions. It was a pretty hard life.

(I was at) Reginald St. School. When we lived in Oxford St. (I remember) the bombs at the back of us, pulling the houses down. We had one of those Anderson Shelters. At night we used to go in this little Anderson Shelter, sit down there waiting until the bombs had gone. There was a big crash in Regent St. where it pulled all the houses down. People got killed. We thought the Germans was coming in our shelter. It used to be really frightening.

The schools decided we should all be evacuated. I was going to go to Australia, but the ships got sunk with a load of children on it. So they decided to take us nearer. I thought I was going miles away – I ended up at Borrowash. We went on this big bus, with our gas masks, to be sorted out. People came out and took us. Mr. and Mrs. Lewis took me and this other girl. It was a lovely big house. We had nice bedrooms which I'd never had – I always slept with me mum.

Borrowash was lovely: you was right out in the country and you had more t' eat, people to look after you, make you clothes. Mrs. Lewis was really kind. She gave us chocolates, things you couldn't get. I used to think that it was the other end of the world, 'cause I'd never been out of Derby. We used to have to walk to Elvaston Castle to do our PE across the fields. Nobody bothered about being cold.

(My mother) came over perhaps once a month on the bus. I was (in Borrowash) about a year. (Then) my mother took ill with this ulcerated leg. She needed somebody to look after her in this little house in Oxford St. It was 1940; I was 13 ½. So I left school and I got my first job at Esme's Hairdressers on Osmaston Rd.

Esme's Hairdresser's, Osmaston Rd

I didn't really (want to do hairdressing) but it was a job; me brother got it me. He said we needed the money. Mum wasn't earning and 13/- a week (65p) sounded like £1300! The hours were terrible - 8.30am to 6pm on your feet – she wouldn't let you sit down. Then (I gave) 10/- (50p) to Mum, 3/- (15p) off for your uniform etc. Mum gave me 2/- (10p) if I was lucky, more often 1/- (5p).

Esme's was a beautiful shop. She'd got this big salon at the front, living accommodation at the back and this big room upstairs where we did all the preparations for the perms. If we wanted the bleach and peroxide stronger we mixed it with a little drop of ammonia – to brighten it up, make your hair blonde. She taught us how to cut; she was very patient.

Perms and Styles in the 40s

Perm solution (in wartime) was hard to get. She used to buy it in great big gallons. It frizzed your hair up for the rest of the year! Perms lasted 6-8 months. (Often) you only wanted one perm a year. They were very strong chemicals; it used to make you feel ill. But we never got chance to be ill, you just went to work. If we hadn't got any work, she sent us down to help people - one on London Rd – we had to clean her house for her. That gave you something to do!

People were poor so they used to run perm clubs. You'd pay in what you could afford, say 1/- or 6d a week, and if you'd got enough people in, you had a draw for a perm (each week) which cost 10/- (50p) or 7/6 (32 ½ p). Everybody got a perm after 6 or 8 weeks.

It took all morning to wind a perm. I wasn't very fast on winding. We had big heavy rollers, bristley, woody things, with a thing on the end (where) you used to put two wires in for electricity. It was all heated. You'd pad them in between so you didn't get heads burnt - if you was neglectful they got burnt heads. Then you were sent upstairs for 2 days to clean all the perm sachets – it was horrible.

Those perms (though), the chemicals killed off any nits! In those days you very rarely got people with nits. (The odd one was) absolutely walking and you don't know until you're half way through. You'd just got to stop what you were doing and explain to the person they'd got "things" in their head. Then you'd sterilise everything, wash the chair, the floor, in case they spread. I think our mums were more careful with us then. You had a nit-night every week when you had a bath and had your hair seen to. Then you had a nit-nurse at school.

We're very lucky here (but) you've got to be more careful. I just take them aside and say," I'm ever so sorry – do you know you've got some lodgers in your hair?" You try to make it as light as you can.

Colouring was very hard and nearly always black. My boss had black, shiny hair and people said they'd like hair like hers. We used Inecto – very strong. It took ages to get out.

Styles mostly were a mass of frizz and Marcelle waves made with irons. Most people had shoulder length hair. (They copied) Hedy Lamarr with her long black hair and "sausage rolls" on top and Betty Grable when you'd got a blonde.

I had to keep the salon clean. We had cubicles – a curtain all round, private. We had to answer the phone. One girl wouldn't answer the phone - she kept calling me from the cubicles. I got behind with me perms and one day I put the phone line round her neck! I got suspended for 3 days and I got a good hiding when I got home, 'cause they stopped all your money.

Smith's Uniforms

I married at 18, Bill Christie in the RAF. When he came out the Forces he just couldn't get a job. I managed to get a part-time job at Smith's, Drewry Lane. I was a cutter, cutting uniforms for the RAF, Army and a lot of Police work. You used big shears – hand cutting. You marked it all out with a pattern, cut it out and it used to make your hands ache. It wasn't well paid; you got a flat rate; over your limit you got a bonus. I used to save all me bonus for more than 10 years. I used to tell everybody I was going to have me own shop. I used to drive them mad. They said, "You'll never get a shop". (But) I just didn't take my bonus; I saved about £900 – a lot of money then.

First Hairdresser's Shop – Rachel's, Uttoxeter Rd.

(I saw) this big double-fronted shop on the corner of Camden St. and Milton St, off Uttoxeter Rd. I talked the owner into letting me have it for 10/- a week. He helped me to do it up and I had it all in blue and gold. It was called "Rachel's", from my sister-in-law, who was marvellous. I stayed at Smith's for another 6 months – I didn't want to let them down – and paid two hairdressers to work whilst I worked weekends and went on all the Wella courses and got my diplomas in perming, colouring, cutting.

Curzon St.

It was all done up beautiful, but after 2 years the landlord got greedy, kept putting the rent up and up. Mrs. Bailey (a hairdresser) came up – she'd heard all the troubles. She asked me if I'd like her shop in Curzon St. The Council owned it and they let me have it for 15/- (75p) a week. Curzon St. was smashing – a great big property. My customers followed me from Milton St. and I've been there for 50 years.

Walker Buildings, Chellaston

My solicitor told me they was building this place up High St. Chellaston (Walker Buildings). She said, "You'll do nothing for the first 5-6 years, but it will be a good shop. You're going into a village and villagers are against outsiders going in." Walker Buildings was just a shell. Frank Innes said I could have it on a peppercorn rent for a year, but I'd have to put my own windows, doors, my own floor – I'd everything to do. It took me nearly a year to get it ready.

Me and the Greengrocers, Pat and Don, was the first in and were the only ones that had done it legally, with Frank Innes. They did their best to try and get me out because my rent couldn't go up very much. Everyone was doubling rents. For the first five years I was only paying about £50 a quarter, for a whole year £200. After, it went up to about £300 and then it stayed at that for 7 years. It was very cheap – they couldn't touch me for 21 years.

Mary Christie's first Chellaston shop, Walker Buildings, Chellaston in the 70s

(The shop was) called Christie's. People wouldn't come because I was new, so for 5-6 years it was hard. I had to coax them in. But I had a good stylist, John, and we did gents as well. John lived above the shop. He worked pretty hard (but) he left me and opened his own shop in Monk St. It's funny – everybody that's worked for me has opened their own shops so I couldn't have been a bad boss. It was hard to get staff to come up and work here and you couldn't get nobody from the village.

After 14 years I decided to start looking (and) got another shop in Baker St. Alvaston. I put (Walker Buildings shop) on the market and this fella came. He wanted it as a video shop. I said there was 7 years left on my lease and he said that'd do him. So he paid me cash and they couldn't touch him for another 7 years.

32 High St.

I said I'd move down here (32 High St.). It was a Beauty Shop then; someone had changed it from the sweety shop to a beauty shop. The Council said all right. I sold my house on Linden Drive and bought it (now Christies'). I still kept Curzon St - sold my Alvaston shop. My son, Tom, came up here. He made a big difference, so I put him in charge. I like it. People have accepted us – we know people. Everybody knows you, talks to you. You feel at home.

32 High St. over the decades:
From top Raynes' Sweet Shop; centre Beauty Salon;
bottom Christies' Hairdressers.

Customers

I've got my favourites. We're pretty lucky. They talk to Tom more than me because he does more in the shop.

People have money problems. You get them who think you're a soft touch: sob story – not enough money to pay you; "Bring it in when you've got it" - you never see them again! They only do it to you once though!

People come in, worried about things and confide in you. Some of the secrets over the years ....it just goes straight through. Tell you they're fed up and going to leave their husband and you try to talk them not to do it. You don't talk about your customers – it's personal. I'd never, never repeat it.

Changes in hairdressing, styles etc

Quickness of perms, all the solutions have changed - not heated - nothing to burn. Perms are milder, softer, chemicals not so strong. – not as good really: don't last long. You're lucky if you get 8 weeks to 3 months now – before it was 5 - 6 months. A perm varies from £25 - £30 (now) – then it was 7/6 (37½ p).

Styles? It's nearly all long hair these days. People rarely ask to look like famous people. They might bring a book in – very rarely a star. Sometimes, "Her hair looked lovely when she was reading the news" – nothing like we used to get: all bubbles and curls and Shirley Temple looks. It's nearly always blonde and highlights, meshes - done with silver foil and you weave it in and out.

(We had) hood dryers (then) - got one in the shop now. We had some on the wall so you could pull it down and put it over the top of their head. As they became a bit moderner, they came on settees and they didn't blow so much – they just had hot air – didn't blow it out. It was nice and warm underneath, sitting there comfortable. Book and cup of tea and they was happy! Ours are on the ceiling now and we pull them down just the same. Not much change.

(It's) not such hard work (now). In those days the bosses were very, very strict. You weren't allowed a radio. Today it's more lackadaisical. Very rare today to get someone dedicated – it's just a job now. Then it was a career – you loved it.

Mary Christie still lives and works at Christies', well past the normal retirement age. Her son, Tom, and grandson work in the shop with her.

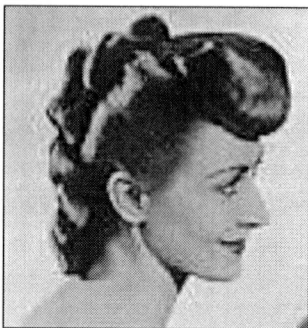

Hairstyles from the 40s to the 70s

HAIRDRESSER – NOW

Mick Whelan

Background

(I was) born in 1965 in Derby. (Dad was) hard working, (a painter and decorator) - worked 6½/7 days a week. We were an Irish Catholic family. I am one of 8 children: 5 brothers and 2 sisters and we didn't have the easiest upbringing. Anyone who has a big family knows it wasn't easy but we were blessed with great parents and felt they gave us a good upbringing.

We lived in a 3 bed semi – me and my 5 brothers shared one bedroom and my 2 sisters had a box room. We were very lucky where we lived in Alvaston, we were able to use the school grounds and play on the condition we looked after the school after hours.

My first (school) was St. John Fishers Primary School on Alvaston St. – 4 or 5 nuns were teaching at the time. There was fantastic discipline, fantastic respect.

Why Hairdressing?

I just had a fascination. My first memory of hairdressing was a lady by the name of Mary and she was on London Rd in Alvaston. All I can remember is this woman in a white coat with a cigarette hanging out the corner of her mouth and smoke rising up into her smoke coloured hair, one eye shut. As years went on we went to a local salon in Alvaston. The owner was Alan Swift. They were very friendly and I liked the idea of it and I felt drawn towards it. At school, I remember the Careers Officer saying, "What do you want to be when you leave school?" I always knew I wanted to be a hairdresser but I daren't ever say it due to the stigma attached to male hairdressing so I basically came up with the macho "I want to be a fireman or an electrician"and not letting anyone know what I wanted to be. My dad felt it was right we should get a career in engineering, so I got an apprenticeship with International Combustion. I remember going into town with my mum to get some clothes, and that's when I first told my mum I did not want to do engineering I actually wanted to do hairdressing.

I saw an advert for a job in town as a hairdresser - went for it, got the job. My mum was 100% behind me saying, "You've got to do what you want to do." I don't think my dad was best pleased - I think he was worried about what sort of career it is. It soon became apparent to him that it was a good job with lots of prospects, kinda quickly realised that with hairdressing you can take it anywhere in the world. You'll never be short of a haircut therefore you will never be short of a pound or two in your pocket.

Career Changes

I started off in Derby city centre. It was a 3 year apprenticeship. It was a very hard training. I remember going in absolutely petrified. We had to wear grey and white uniforms. We had to wear a tie and I just remember shaking like a leaf. It was Monday 26th August 1982, 9 o'clock start. I think I was there at five past eight. I daren't be late – it was instilled in us. It was very exciting. It was a great new world. The wages were very poor - I started off on £29.50 - literally less than £1 an hour.

I felt the training at the time wasn't the best training in the world. It was all done in-house, so we never ever went to college, no paperwork done whatsoever, so when you are doing a certain style you knew how to do it because you were shown how to do it but you didn't know why or why you were doing it this particular way. It was a lot of natural ability what got you through.

(I worked) in Derby, Manchester and Scunthorpe. I got made redundant (and) went to work at Rolls Royce in Derby, doing gents hairdressing part-time, travelling from Sheffield to Derby on a regular basis for about 3 years. I was a vibro-polisher at PCF, Precision Castings Facility in Sinfin. It's a great place to work, the money was brilliant but it just wasn't me. I can't do the mundane, going to the same machines, doing the same kind of job. Hairdressing you are meeting new people, you are meeting customers, different personalities, every day. I always felt drawn to that.

By then I had this 2/3 year plan to save up and get back into hairdressing and do it by myself.

Setting up shop in Chellaston

Mick Whelan's shop, Walker Buildings, High St. Chellaston 2012

Some money came from my ex-employer, (some from) doing gents hairdressing part-time. (Then) I heard they were doing redundancies at Royce's, so I took redundancy - that was another lump sum of money that helped me. The year 2000, my brother, Pat, who is now my business partner, said, "Oh, there is a need for a hairdresser in Chellaston, a gents hairdresser."

So I came back to Derby to have a look at Chellaston one or two times, looked outside to see what the passing trade was like, went to Roman House in Derby, got all the info about how many houses in Chellaston and what was happening development - wise and basically I could not believe it, there was not a gents hairdresser in Chellaston. So we swiftly moved and got the shop, where we are today, 51 High Street. Before, it was a fruit and veg. shop. We had to completely gut it. We started with a blank canvas. I wanted good quality gents' hairdressers. We did a 5,000 leaflet campaign telling customers who I was, where I'd come from and my idea. It's £10 here for a haircut; you go into town nowadays and for a working gent it's £15/20. I wanted to bring the city centre out to the suburbs. I think we have brought a smart, modern style of shop, with modern and traditional ideas. I'm traditionally trained; I'm modern trained, so I can do the classic short back and sides for the elderly gentlemen and the modern haircuts - punk rocker to the Mohican.

We opened up in July 10th 2000 and my mum was the honorary person to cut the ribbon. It was more a proud moment for her rather than us. She did believe in me, that one day I would get my own shop in the hairdressing world. I love the place. I'm glad I came here. Businesswise, I think it is a lovely village We do want to put something back in the community – (we're) not just here to take your money and run.   We are linked with Swarkestone Cricket Club, Chellaston Senior School, Homefields and Chellaston Juniors. We are also linked with various charities: Prostate Cancer, Breast Cancer - something we deal with every year. I am a great believer in it. I definitely believe (businesses) should put something back in.

75

Health hazards of the job (Mick only does gents' hair now to avoid chemical products).

In the 80s, they were talking about the ozone layer and it was causing damage, all these hairsprays, the bleaches, the peroxides and perm solutions especially. The perms were a massive business.   You were working in a salon with 20/30 staff working in there and you could easily have 5/10 perms on the go, so exposure to chemicals was quite high. I developed asthma through the chemicals of the ladies' hairdressing (world) and I just had so much time off. I went through a state for a few years when I was quite ill with it.   I got pneumonia twice; I got bronchial problems, got breathing problems.   I went through a real tough period. I had to leave hairdressing almost.

The hairdressing body or the government changed some of the products - changed some of the chemicals to protect the ozone layer. Loads of hairdressers, even today, now use inhalers. I have got 5 or 6 staff with me at the moment and 3 are using inhalers and it's all through hairdressing. They say with asthma if you get it as a child you grow out of it, get it as an adult you have it for life. So you learn to live with it.

Repetitive strain is a problem with holding the comb in a certain way.   I have had my carpel tunnel done on my left hand. I have heard of people get bone conditions and things like that. I have been very lucky over the years. We've got a friend in the family who literally had to pack up hairdressing because of it. She cannot cut hair because of injury to her hand and it's all through hairdressing.

We do a lot more gents than ladies. To do a ladies' hairstyle could take up to an hour; if you do a gent it's like 10/15mins. So you are doing 4 times as many haircuts as the ladies are and because of the amount of gents I do, at the age of 47 this year, I do feel my hands stiffening up – so it is a concern.   You get a lot of back problems but that goes down to how you were shown when you were young. You get a lot of knee problems, I've had a little sciatica problem but nothing major. I've seen hairdressers fall by the wayside due to the injuries.

Changes in Hairstyles 1980s to today

I started hairdressing 1982 - the New Romantic years.   You got people like Duran Duran, Depeche Mode, Wham, Boy George, all them sort of groups – it was a massive following. The men started growing their hair long at the back. In 1980s there was highlighted hair and that scene exploded – there were men coming in having capped highlights all the time. There were the famous perms at the back for men. Football icons as well - the Kevin Keegan, Chris Waddell look. People look towards icons even today, 30 years later, coming in saying, "Can we have it like Justin Bieber? " (In) my dad's day, it was the Tony Curtis look. We are still using pop stars and football players - everyone, of course, wants the image.

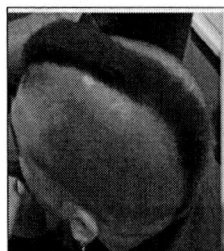

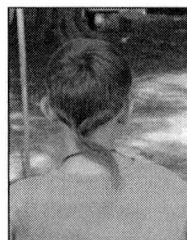

The famous one of all time is David Beckham. He is one of the most copied stars I have ever known. From the years he started football he had the classic centre parting with a floppy fringe that was copied all over the place. He had it highlighted - the highlighting world went absolutely crazy. When he shaved it all off, allegedly it cost the hairdressing industry 50 million pounds, because of people losing money highlighting. A gent coming to a salon wanted to pay £30/40 for a set of highlights and a cut; all of a sudden he had it shaved off for £5 so the hairdressing industry lost nearly £50m.

One or two people who don't quite look like David Beckham! - or their hair texture is quite different. (If) they have very curly hair, to have a straight hairstyle is quite difficult. You have to be realistic. If we've got a picture we know what you're thinking of. Twenty or thirty years (ago) we had style books where you had your bog standard styles. Today you can go on the internet and get millions of pictures; it's really changed over the years. We've had some amazingly strange requests. Nothing shocks me anymore - 80s perms, shaven sides, the Mohican. We've had the undercut where it was shaved underneath and the hair flopped over the top.

Now we're having men having hair shaved from one side across the back to another side. So it's a diagonal shaving where the rest of it is all spiked up. We're having fringes shaved out of the way at the moment. We're having patterns put into the hair - things like lines, zigzags. We don't do words but we do things like the Ram, if someone's got a favourite football team – but that is a more specialist thing now. Customers know exactly what they want now - more confident, more conscious of the look, of the style, of the way they are.

When I was young you would hardly dare to talk to the hairdresser - I remember going for a haircut and daren't say a word. Kids are more confident today - more vocal. Now you have 4/5/6 year olds who know exactly what they want. "Can I have it shaven at the back, mate?" "Can I have a Mohican, can I have some colour on it?" We have some fun colour sprays we spray on peoples' hair; it washes out. We try and treat the kids as what we treat the adults, with a little bit of respect.

It would be unprofessional to do something (that) someone is asking for and you know that is not going to suit. We had a young boy, who goes to a local school, and wanted a proper shaved Mohican. His mum wasn't sure and I said," Well, personally, I think the school won't take too kindly to it," and I had a chat with the boy. I gave him a similar sort of style but without the proper Mohican because I feel he would have been suspended, and cost a lot of stress.

Customer care, medical problems

The thing, hopefully, about hairdressing, you need to be compassionate, somebody who can listen - it's a great quality. You do get a lot of people telling their problems. You get marriage break-ups, people who do not know what to do - work things, personal problems in regard to illnesses.

Over the 12 years we've been open we know of 4 people we referred to the doctors. I personally spotted a couple of chaps where I've seen little growths on the back (of the head) and I've noticed it over the year and thought it got a bit bigger - check it out - and all these people have been told they have (some form of) cancer. It's part of our job. We are on top of the head, we can see it a lot closer - notice anything unusual going on, on the scalp. You get to know people suffering from cancers and things; you get attached to these people and sadly they pass away – that's very hard, very sad.

(Nit infestation) was big in the 80s. All went very quiet in the 90s – it was still around but nowhere like now; we are seeing it on a weekly basis. The sad thing is there is treatments out there. It's very simple (and) inexpensive to deal with. Unfortunately, there are still people who don't treat it, leave it and it just goes round and round in circles. If somebody comes in and we see nits or eggs we don't cut their hair because it is just going to pass the infestation through the shop. We do it very discreetly, explain the treatment available.

Running the salon

I've seen some fantastic hairdressers who are amazing haircutters, who've got great skill but the businesses have failed simply because today you're not just a hairdresser you are an accountant, you're a health and safety officer, you're a mediator with your staff. You're a counsellor, you're a book keeper, a receptionist - you are everything. You have got to have so many skills it's unbelievable. It is very, very hard and I totally respect anybody who is running any business.

I am the first there in the morning. I like to get there for 8 o'clock in the morning. I like to have a solid hour before I open and that gives me time to do any paperwork, catch up with the errands I have to do that day, any meetings I've got to sort out and it's the same thing at night. All the girls go home first and I am the last one left. It is very difficult, but that's where a great team comes in. I've got a great business partner, my brother; he is not a hairdresser, and he's fantastic with all the background things - staff wages, rules, taxation, all the paperwork, end of year taxes, VAT.

The very first day I opened, I was by myself; it took time to build staff. We have got some amazing staff now. Then we've got a fantastic manageress, Emma. She's been with us now for 8½ years. Absolutely amazing person, a great hairdresser and 100% relied on so if I do want to take a holiday or I take a day off, I know I can leave the shop in her hands.

Wages, Expenses, Tips

We pay well above minimum wage but it's all on experience. (Scissors are) very expensive. People's jaw drops open when they realise what we pay; they have got it into their head it's like a £10/£20/£30 pair. I use Japanese scissors. We regard them in the hairdressing world as probably one of the best in the world. They are made of cobalt making them waterproof. Mine are self – serrated edge and the particular ones I am using at the moment are £265 + VAT. My second pair are a similar price. One of our girls has (a) £300+ set at the moment and they go way up to hundreds of pounds. We know people who have spent £500 on them.

(Tips) is a tough one. Obviously (stylists) regard it a top up to their wages. I know people say it is your job and yes, they are absolutely right. We don't expect it all the time. I do it myself if I go to a restaurant or somewhere where I feel I got exceptional service, taxi services, what have you. People appreciating what you have done - it's a nice gesture at the end if someone gives you one. You really appreciate it.

FARMER – THEN

Donald Barker

Donald has been a long standing member of Chellaston History Group. He grew up on his family's farm, End Farm at Sinfin and lived there from 1927 to 1961. He has many valuable memories of farm working life.

Early years

I was born in 1925 at the Nightingale Home, Derby, with a twin, Peter. The nurse that nursed my mother, when she was in the hospital, married my father a year later after my mother had died. (Father had) a lot to do – farming. It was a bit difficult for him. There wasn't a lot of love, as a lot of ideal fathers have. (It was) even more difficult for my step-mother. The oldest youngster was about 15 or 16. It must have been so sad for them, losing their mother like that. How my (step-mother) managed – I don't know.

The farmhouse

Our farm was on the corner down (what is now) Redwood Rd - all houses now. (The farmhouse) was mid Victorian, or a bit older. It consisted of a big farm kitchen with blue bricks for the floor. The parlour had got oak beams in it. There'd be 4 bedrooms and a landing where there was a huge picture of Edward VII and Queen Alexandra and two great big barn owls in glass cases on my mother's dower chest. We also had a glass case with a little red squirrel, stuffed. My bedroom had a kind of concrete floor and a fireplace in it. No central heating, nothing like that. And believe you me when you'd got cold winters – 1947, oh it was cold!

We had oil lamps. Some were made of brass and some of glass. They were very ornate. We didn't have electricity until about 1937 or 38. It was a great occasion.

Water was from a well – the pump was in the kitchen with a big metal handle you moved up and down to get the water. It was lovely water and it came into what you call the slopstone, a big sink, but when you came to wash the pots up the water was very hard. There was no such thing as soap in those days – we had soda and of course that was no good for your hands. On the other side of this sink there was another, smaller, pump – that was for soft water. If it was dry weather it would dry up and you couldn't use it – no more rainwater would come. If you used that to wash your hair, it was like washing your hair in silk!

Fortunately in our bedroom we had a bath - a proper bath – we were very modern - and a lead pipe going through the wall and the water went down, but we had to carry the water up. We hotted it up in the copper in this big kitchen and then we carried the water up the stairs. When we were little we had a zinc bath and we used to have our bath by the fire.

There was one toilet for the visitors – you had to go up the path in the front garden to it and it was a wooden one - a two-seater. Of course we had to empty it now and then - everybody did. Oh my word, that job was awful! We also had one over in the yard what we used to use regularly. After the war we did get a WC. We thought that was absolutely marvellous. The greatest invention, in my life is the WC.

The farm

(It was) a crops and dairy farm, rented from a butcher - Turner his name was, of Mill Hill Lane. He used to have a lot to do with what they called the 'Iron Tent,' a Non-Conformist Church at the top of Normanton Rd. He was very religious. He wasn't a bad landlord.

Because the landlord ran this church, all the children used to come down, every Whit Tuesday, on Offilers Brewery's carts with the horses pulling them, all decorated up, and they used to have their games and tea on our land. We used to think that was lovely and we were let join in with them – we used to love that.

We'd got my brothers and we used to employ two men. One lived in the town in the West End – he was a proper character, old Frank Ryde. I remember once, he was cleaning ditches out and when he'd got all the sludge out – eels galore! I never had any, but Frank used to take them home for his family. Mother cut them up and fried them in pieces in the frying pan on top of the fire - they were like snakes. I never had any, I didn't fancy it but they were a delicacy.

I started (working on the farm) when I was about 17. But I was just dog's body, you might say, with my brothers being older. I had no trouble getting up – about 6 o'clock. It was Peter's (turn) one week, me another week. When the animals were living in the sheds in the winter it was our job to go round all the three or four sheds to see that their beds were all clean.

The farmyard at End Farm, Sinfin

We were all very particular about looking after the animals – get any muck off and shake the bedding, see that it was nice and dry for them. We did have sheep for a time but we had to pack that up because they were mauled to death. There used to be dogs from the new estates would come and worry them and we found them in an empty pit – no end of the sheep all lying dead.

At Christmas during the war we used to do a lot of poultry, turkeys etc to sell. It was hard work. Geese, ducks were very hard to pluck because there was the outer feather and then down inside to keep it waterproof. You got quite good at it and you didn't tear the skin. And then dressing them – I could do that.

Work in the fields

One of the things I thought was back-breaking was what they called 'singling' in Spring, about April/May time – you had to hoe the lines of mangols and turnips and we used to stack them. My brothers were older than me and especially my brother, John, he worked and he worked and he worked. John was forward-looking, modern, where father was old - fashioned.

We used to grow all our own vegetables. We used to grow cabbages as well - always used to win at Brailsford Ploughing Match and West Hallam Ploughing match.

My eldest brother was a champion hedge-cutter – he's won cups galore. My brothers were very keen on growing chrysanthemums and sweet peas and showing them at the King's Hall in Derby.

Harvest

We liked autumn because when we'd done all the harvesting and all the hard work, we could start going to dances again. There'd be Harvest Festival at church – and they always got us farmers' sons to read lessons – I read one of the lessons from the book of Deuteronomy. I had a job to get that out! There was the decorating of the church – in those days with sheaves of corn. When they started having combines there wasn't any sheaves.

We didn't have combine harvesters like they have now. It was the binder and either the tractor or horses. With a binding machine there was long knives that would go down. It would go round and pick the corn up and throw it down, fastened with a string automatically. After they'd cut the corn, we had to get these sheaves and put them all up into stooks, about 12 sheaves to a stook. Sometimes if there was thistles in it the thistles would get on your legs terrible.

The harvest was a lovely time – the weather was often lovely in the Autumn and you'd be cutting the hedges. Then there'd be Bonfire Night to look forward to with the great big pile of hedge cuttings.

The dairy side

It would be all hand milking and it was hard work. But then when we got the milking machines that was OK – but you had to keep them all clean – that was my job. We had a steriliser in a great big cabinet and we had to sterilise everything and bottle the milk.

I used to take the milk round on a horse and float in Sinfin and quite a few places in town. How on earth it was worth the round, I don't know, taking it right into town. We had a car later on and my sister used to drive it and take the milk in it, but I've been with father right up Ashbourne Road delivering quarts and pints of milk. We used to go and have our bit of lunch sometimes in a pub called 'The Gallant Hussar.' I'd have a drink of lemonade and he'd have his pint and I used to think I was living it up

When we first started, we sold milk loose. We'd use a churn and pour it out into a 2 gallon bucket with a handle on. Your true measures, the pint and the quart would be in there and you'd ladle it out. The customers would have bowls or jugs to put it in. Some of them weren't particular – they'd have a job to keep it from going sour in the summer. We used bottles from about 1938.

When a cow had calved we used to have the wheelbarrow ready with straw in it to take the calf from the cow. We'd put it in this barrow and take it into a little shed that was just for calves. It was a bit cruel to take it from the mother straight away. But that's how we did it.

When the cows had their calves, their milk, called beastings, was very rich – to get the calves going. I used to bottle that and give it to the customers – some of them loved it. It made custard just like egg custard only I don't think you had to put any eggs in it - it was that rich. It was very nice with nutmeg on top.

Donald with the dairy herd 1945/6. Farm cottages in the background.

Donald with the milk float and pony, "Peggy" c.1956

Donald and "Peggy", the milk-round horse in the farmyard at End Farm. (Now built on)

GOOD WORKMANSHIP.

This fine stack of Yeoman Wheat on the Farm of Mr. C. Barker, Sinfin End, Derby, built and thatched by his son John on the left.

The farm's prize-winning wheat stack

Killing the pig

We used to kill a pig twice a year. Especially during the war it was very helpful for rationing. Killing the pig was a major effort. We had an old man; he used to go round the farms killing pigs for people like us. Tommy Wilkinson his name was – a proper character. He had a humane gun.

I had a special job. After he'd shot the pig, he'd slit the throat and let the blood come out. I had to hold the big enamel bowl under and be sure and get all the blood in it and, with a wooden spoon, keep stirring it so it didn't congeal. That was used for making the black puddings. They consisted of pearl barley, chopped leeks and pieces of fat from the pig's stomach. It was very nice.

After the pig had been shot he was put onto a bench and we'd scald it with hot, scalding water and then we'd scrape all the hair off. Then Tommy would get cutting it. There was such a lot you could make from the pig. The white stomach lining was called the leaf – you'd get that out, peel it off and cut it up. That'd make your lard - hot it up on the range and it would melt it. You'd let it go cold, then that would be for lard.

After it had been cooked, there was pieces left over – they used to go nice and crispy and they were called chitterlings. They used to sell them in the butchers' shops before the war. They were very tasty, I liked those.

Stepmother used to boil the head for ages. Then with a knife pick all the meat out of the head, put it in basins and put the old flat iron on to press it. When it was cold you'd turn it out and you'd got like a Christmas pudding shape and that was called brawn – that was very tasty too. I remember my Great Aunt Harriet coming from Hilton to make the sausages and pork pies for us. They had a car! She thought she was the grand lady – she was really.

Market day

The Market was all centred round the Corporation Hotel. I went sometimes with father in the horse and trap. You could take your horse out of the float and put it in the stabling in the Central Stables on Cockpit Hill - like people can put cars in a car park now. They'd always end up in the Corporation Hotel – sometimes have a drop too much! I remember going there when the Groom family kept it.

Trips to Chellaston

During the war - I'd only be 14, 15 or 16 (I used to go through Chellaston) on my pony to my cousin's at Weston–on-Trent. My parents would go in the pony and trap from Sinfin before we had a car. Chellaston, like everywhere else, wasn't developed then. We'd come over Sinfin Moor, through Sinfin Moor Lane, into the High Street, up where the plaster pits were, through the plaster pit area and then onto the gravel track to Weston Fields Farm. I enjoyed going.

It was a similar farm to ours – they sold milk and had corn crops for the animals. I think they had to take the milk down the gravel road to the road in Chellaston for the Co-op lorry to pick it up in 10 gallon churns.

Great Aunt Lil Hollingsworth was mother of 2 men and 2 women who farmed it, all bachelors and spinsters. They were an eccentric lot. I'd put my pony in the stable there, then I liked talking to my great aunt Lil. She used to sit there all in black – a long black skirt - in a rocking chair and tell me tales about how things were years ago. They were good cooks. One day we had jugged hare and it was absolutely lovely, and blackcurrant jam with it and the vegetables – lovely. The big entertainment was farm suppers.

Sometimes I'd go and stay there. One night the fox had got into the hens. My cousin Daisy was yelling her head off because this fox had got the poultry. She'd got a double-barrelled shot gun - she was as good a shot as any man.

Changes at End Farm – move to Combustion

(Sinfin, when we moved there,) was a very small place. It was just a little hamlet, consisting of two cottages, the little farm across the road and then our farm. And across a trackway at the side of Summers' farm, you went to what you call the Poplars Farm – Ted Moult's home before Scaddows Farm in TIcknall.

We only rented our farm and the landlord sold a great patch of our plough land and pasture land that is all built on now. The first lot he sold, they had the council houses built – what they call old Sinfin now. And then just before the war in 1938 he sold some more of our land on the right hand side, and that's called the Sunshine Estate and all that was built on. This considerably lessened our land.

My father said he was going to retire in 1961. We all had to find other jobs. Luckily we knew one of the bosses at Combustion and we all got a job on Sinfin Lane.

A huge contrast! Noise! I was mate to a millwright. A mucky job, but interesting - keeping the millwright's tools clean and handing them to him.

When I first went I didn't know the difference between a hammer and a chisel! One thing I noticed - swearing, language! To keep overhead cranes going we had to go up a steel ladder at the end of each wall. I was frightened to death! Cleaning the oil tank out of the loco that pushed the steel wagons – Oh dear! I was thin and so I did it. I was black as the ace of spades! (It was) better pay - about £15 per week – double that I got on the farm; and there was a happier atmosphere and not such long hours.

FARMER – NOW

Ed Hicklin

The Hicklins – a farming family

I'm the 4th generation farmer. Grandad's father, my great grandfather, bought White House Farm. They used to live at the bottom of where Raynesway is now and they had a milk round. When Raynesway was built, the house was knocked down and that's when they came to Chellaston. It was a traditional mixed farm, 100 acres or so then (which) now certainly wouldn't support a family on a mixed farming basis, let alone support employing people as well. He grew potatoes, he'd got chickens, he'd got pigs, they grew sugar beet and fodder beet because you'd got your horses; you'd got to grow feed for your horses, so a percentage of your ground was kept for your horses straightaway.

My grandad would have perhaps half a dozen people working for him. Historically, you wouldn't have a 500 acre arable farm. One team of horses and one man could plough one acre in a day, so that gives you some indication of what sort of scale you'd be talking about. Your mixed farm would spread the workload evenly throughout the year. I've got friends that are farming 1000 or 1200 acres on their own now. So they would have had contractors come and do the combining and they'd do the carting.

Dad's 71 now. He enjoys what he does and I suspect he will carry on doing it until he can't. He's worked really hard all his life - all he wanted to do is be in the fields and make stuff grow.

My grandparents lived in White House Farm, where Dad was brought up and we lived in a house in High Street, so it wasn't growing up on the farm as such. We had beef cattle so as I got older, there'd be a lot of time spent in school holidays and in the winter feeding the cattle, making sure they'd got plenty of water and clean beds.

I was in the teens when I started getting more involved. We grew the crops as well, so in the summer holidays, we'd be out harvesting, planting and doing the timely jobs.

Starting to drive the tractor

I was about 10 or 11 (when I started driving the tractor) around the yards. You have to be 14 to be on a tractor now. I remember taking my tractor driving test when I was 16 to drive on the road. I took my tractor test in the middle of Derby at the test centre. I took my little tractor into the middle of town on London Road. I passed, so I was on the road from when I was 16.

Last farm in Chellaston

We're certainly the last farm in Chellaston (we have no land left in Chellaston, only White House Farm buildings where Dad still lives; we are one of only a few left in the city). We farm about 500 acres in 6 parishes: Aston on Trent, Swarkestone, Shardlow, Barrow on Trent and Weston and Sinfin - that's probably part of the city, round the Sinfin Moor, and some in the city, round by Rolls-Royce. We own not quite half of the land we farm, the rest we rent from 3 landlords: Derby Diocesan Board, Bellways Developers and another biggish chunk is the Harpur Crewe Estate.

It's almost exclusively arable now. We had beef cattle but, with the foot and mouth epidemic in 2001 we were impacted by regulations - the restrictions on movement. Nowadays all cattle have to have a passport that follows them wherever they go. Animals maintain the green and pleasant landscape but on the urban fringe, fences aren't always respected. People walking their dogs sometimes think they've got a right to go through, so the phone could ring at 2 and 3 o'clock in the morning, "Cows are out on the road on the A6," and you would have to go and try and shepherd them back in as best you can.

I couldn't see cattle making the reward to justify the work, so we've gone down the arable route; while we miss the stock, it's reduced our workload.

The farming year

In the winter we employ 1 man and we endeavour to keep him busy by doing maintenance. We're tidying up, maintaining, getting things ready, so that when we want them we're like a coiled spring ready to go. It's also a bit more leisure time with the family or hobbies, go on holiday or decorate - bits and pieces that normal people would do at the weekend. I'm on the parish Council in Aston so I perhaps get a little bit more involved in the winter than I would in the summer.

In March the crops are just starting to come out of winter, so we're starting to feed, check that there's no disease or weed problem. When we plant the fields our machinery that we feed and weed the ground with is 21 metres wide so those "tram lines" you see in the fields are 21 metres apart. Then when we drive up and down the fields to feed and spray granular nitrogen, potash and phosphate we're not overlapping or missing anything.

Weed control

We use Round-up, which is a very commonly available product that's been around for a long time - I've seen people drink that, which, I'm sure, is a bit of a party trick. It's a really good way of weed control and one of the safest. You're putting on perhaps a litre of Round-up to the hectare so in terms of volume it's a tiny amount that does the trick. It's a non-specific: you spray it on the ground, anything green it hits, it will die. But as soon as it hits the soil it's inert, it's harmless.

Pesticides and pests

(We use pesticides) as little as possible. Years ago farms used to just have a blanket spray because spray was cheap. They didn't realise quite what the impact then was; we're so much more environmentally aware now and I am no longer qualified to decide what we spray. I have to employ an agronomist. It drives me nuts, because no-one knows the land like we do. We could spend perhaps £10000 or £12000 a year on pesticides. It's a big cost, it's bizarre. Some of the chemicals we use are at such low volumes. We put on 120 litres of water to the hectare, which isn't much and into that we'll perhaps put 200ml of chemical. The quality of the spray that we put on has to be so good because the actual concentrate is parts per million.

We handle it with gloves and masks on a hard standing. It's a lot less toxic than it used to be in the 70s; now it looks quite innocuous stuff. It aggravates me that we get a bad press and on the TV. People don't seem to understand that if we ruin the environment on our farm, the crops aren't going to survive. We want the best compromise for land and for the worms. They're essential to the ground, so we're not going to beggar about with them.

We get more pigeons now than ever, but they're actually breeding oil seed rape with a bitter taste so the pigeons don't like it. We've got gas guns to keep the pigeons away - basically a tube, a spark and a bottle of propane and every hour it will go bang. We put the gas gun in a heavy steel lock box so that people can't damage or destroy them, and take them on the little tractor. The ones that we've got have got light sensors: they start a couple of hours after daylight; as soon as it goes dark they stop. It's odd, the smaller birds don't seem as bothered, the thrushes and the sparrows they don't seem to move but pigeons... I suppose pigeons by their nature are a little bit more nervy and they do go.

Slugs, I don't know where slugs have come from in the last 10 years. Slugs never used to be a problem but now, across the whole farm and everyone you talk to, slugs are an issue. We only put perhaps 3 kilos of slug pellets to the hectare.

No more ploughing

We've changed recently. We've invested in a new system where we don't plough any more. We go through the combine - either chop the straw back on to the ground or take it off for animal bedding, let the flush of weeds grow that come out from behind the combine, go over with a low dose of Round-up, because the young plants are very easy to kill, and then we go straight in with this machine and it plants the seed straight into the soil as the combine left it.

This year, by using that system, we've saved about 10000 or 12000 litres of diesel in terms of not having to plough, rotavate or condition the soil. We've just gone straight in with this fairly simple piece of kit. There are 9 legs; it works a little bit of soil where the seed goes and sets the seed in a 6 inch band and has a 3 metre working width. Claydon, who make the machine, are based in Norfolk. They've been using it on their 2000 acre farm exclusively for the last 10 years and their farm looks as well as any I've been on. They argue that the soil structure is improved because you're not turning the whole lot up - you're letting nature (do the work). Our soil structure now is very good. I've not sold my plough, we've still got all the equipment in the shed, should things change, but when I look at the amount of hours and the diesel, and in terms of the environment, 10000 litres of diesel saving is fantastic.

The trouble is, when you go with this system, once you've planted the field, it looks awful. Dad hates it. He likes to see nice brown soil, flat, firm and level with fine straight rows of crop growing into the horizon; this, perhaps for 2 months after you've set it, it just looks awful because we've got this god-awful looking battlefield. Slugs love that, because it's lumpy, it's open and there's plenty of places for them to hide. I would think this year we've lost perhaps an acre, an acre and a half which I can attribute exclusively to slugs. (That cost us) perhaps £500. When we used to plough and cultivate slugs don't like a nice fine, firm seedbed, so that wasn't a problem.

We're perhaps one of the first around here to adopt this system. It was a big leap of faith to go, especially with wheat, commodity prices rising as they were at the time. We could have had a crop failure but, as things stand now, the whole farm looks magnificent, if I say so myself! So time will tell.

Our 4 crops

The crops that we grow now are oilseed rape, winter wheat, winter barley and some linseed. They will all grow on heavy Chellaston clay. The heavy clay, you can't make a fine soil. If you've any in your gardens people will know that when it's wet you just can't go near it. If you manage it well, it is the best for growing. It's really strong land and there's plenty of nutrition and feed in it and it holds the moisture. So, if, in April, May time, we get a drought period the clay ground will cope much better than the land at Swarkestone that is on sand.

Our cropping as a whole is all to do with the rotation - resting and recuperation of land. Oilseed rape actually fixes nitrogen at its roots. In any given year we've got between 100 and 150 acres of rape. It came along In the 70s. It's an oil based crop. We sell it to the crushers and they extract the oil from it, for biodiesel or for margarine. Pure rapeseed oil is coming through now as it's low in oleic acid or fats; McDonalds now use it exclusively. It's the least bad fat for cooking. It's become so popular in the UK because you can harvest it with your regular combine. We desiccate it to accelerate the ripening process then go straight in with the combine.

(Our) winter wheat is specifically feed wheat, animal grade. It doesn't go for bread making flour, it goes to feed livestock.

Nearly all the barley that we grow goes to a cattle farmer in Stafford; we've cut out all the merchants and the agents and sell direct to him.

Linseed - it's the beautiful blue you occasionally see just after the yellow rape has flowered. It's the most beautiful blue colour. It just looks like water when it's there. It's a lovely crop. Linseed is quite a useful product. It can be for human consumption. You can sprinkle it on your Weetabix in the morning if you want to - It has got a lovely flavour. We've grown it at Swarkestone, at the back of the Crewe and Harpur and we've grown it at Ambaston. We grow it on a contract for a firm in Belgium. For the last few years it has gone on a lorry to their processing plant.

Linseed is planted in the spring, so by planting 50 acres of linseed it takes 50 acres out of the pressure of the workload in the autumn. This year we've not planted any. We managed to get everything planted in the autumn, which was really good. In 2007, we had the dreadfully wet harvest. We had linseed at Swarkestone all just about ready to harvest, June, July and the whole bally field flooded and the water washed all the seed pods away. Unbelievable! We'd gone from expecting 80 tonnes of linseed off this field, we got 7. A loss of £24,000.

Harvest

July we're moving into harvest. Because of the variety of crops we grow, they ripen at different times. It's lovely. To actually, after months of inactivity, get on and do something is a joy. The harvest is the bit that demonstrates to you how well you've done your job. The crops can have looked great all year but until you get the combine in and start taking the wheat off the field, that's when you know how good or badly you've done.

Usually, there's sun shining, which always makes things better. So in a 10 day period we can get the rape harvest done and then that allows us to clear the ground and start ready for planting the next crop. Move on to the barley and then the wheat's ready and that takes you through to the end of August.

It needs to be less than 15% moisture content and we've got a machine that can test for that. (Then we) just tip it straight into the store and blow cold air through it because, if you can store wheat at 15% and less than 15 degrees C it will store in a heap, for a couple of years and it won't deteriorate. We try not to harvest any at more than 19% or 19½%, because to take that 4% of moisture out (we have to use the) grain drying plant at Dad's. It's a very elderly piece of kit; it works but you're burning diesel, it's labour intensive, you can't leave it alone, someone needs to be managing it, moving the grain from A to B to C before you can get it into the store.

Dad and I do the combining and carting between us. Our combine's got a 17 foot working width and you can travel at sort of 5 miles an hour, so you're covering some ground. On a nice day, 35 to 40 acres is achievable. They're great machines. I sit on the combine and Dad shuttles the trailers back to the yard.

You tend not to go out with a combine until nearly lunchtime because we let the dew burn off. (We work until) 10 or 11 o'clock at night because, if we're going through to that time of night the dew hasn't started to come down and you're making best use of it. The puddle of light round the combine, it's almost daylight in the little sphere where you work. We have gone later if the weather forecast is not great. There are some times when you just can't wait. If it's warm and wet for any length of period, once that seed has ripened it will start to germinate and the feed people don't want plants, they want seed!

Tractors

We've got 3 older, not quite vintage, but 20 year-old tractors, yard tractors. We use a little one for running round. We've got 3 modern tractors. Until recently one would pull the drill, one would pull the plough and one would do the cultivation work. (They are) on the smaller side nowadays. It looks jolly big when you see it driving past but there are far bigger. Our biggest tractor is 150 horse power and the list price of it will be perhaps £100,000. We would keep that 3 or 4 years. We tend to have Massey Fergusons because there's a reasonable local dealer at Fauld at Tutbury.

We've got nice, modern machinery because we spend a lot of time sitting on it and you want a nice environment to work in. The last one we bought has 3 computers on it - a whole bank of instruments that monitor the fuel it's using, the amount of wheel slip that's involved and the big electro-hydraulic system. The accelerator is driven electronically whereas on the other tractors there's rods and levers that operate the valves and pumps. It's climate controlled so there's air conditioning and heating, like in your car. There's a big filtration system so that you're not getting any of the dust or the pollen or any of the chemicals coming into the cab. It's a sealed bubble.

We've got a heated, air suspension seat - they're really nice; you spend an awful lot of time sat on it. There's the stereo. There are fridges in them. A lot take their sandwiches with them and keep going. We don't work terribly far from home; we'll (usually) come home (to eat).

You can't have noisy places to work, so the one that we've got has got a jockey seat in it so you can have a passenger in it and you can converse (easily). We don't bother with ear protectors any more. You could go to work in a clean suit, tie. As long as nothing broke or needed adjusting, you could sit there all day doing the dirtiest of jobs and come home clean. (I just wear) jeans, shirt. You don't need layers and layers of clothes on, as you did in Dad's day, because it's like a modern day workplace.

Above and below: harvesting off Snelsmore Lane, at the rear of Ed's farmhouse.

Our Combine

(We only use it for) 6 weeks a year. We looked at contractors (but) the contractor's got a big acreage to do and because of the weather windows and you want the 15% moisture we can pick and choose when we go. Ours is a small combine; the ones that you see the contractors have, they're anything up to half a million quid because they've got satellite technology on them and they steer themselves.

The combine we've got now is 3 years old, a New Holland machine made in Belgium - 300 horse power, 6.5 litre engine. They're about £140,000. The drive, the gearing, it's all oil. It will use about 30 litres an hour of fuel so I will put 400 or 450 litres of diesel in it in a morning. I bought 5000 litres of red, agricultural diesel on Monday and I paid 61p per litre for it – we get the VAT back. It's 68p a litre today.

There's no heater in it because when you're out with the combine it should be nice sunny weather. It's got a fantastic air conditioning system in it, really good flood lights all the way round so you can see what's going on and on ours there's a camera on it so you can see what's happening at the back, much like the construction lorries.

Health and safety

Everything has danger but you take a common sense approach. If you've got a piece of machinery and the belt's stuck or something, I suppose you take a balanced risk. I wear good boots with toe protectors because that's common sense.

You're a little more removed now - the combine we've got, you're in the safe environment of the cab; if you get off the seat the engine stops. (But) you can't guard the working bits of it because you've got to go into the crop. Dad lost his arm 40 years ago so it's been brought home a little more closely.

If you've got mouldy grain because you've not conditioned it or kept it in the right climate then you get the condition farmer's lung because all the spores blow off it.

I hold a PA1 and PA2 in chemical handling and management. The certificate is run by the National Professional Training Council. There's courses to go on and on-going training. You don't just take a test and forget about it. You need to accrue points over a period of time; it's all linked into a database and every 18 months you get a statement to say you either need to do more or you've got sufficient.

Other rules and regulations

The Environment Agency, Natural England, (make it) mandatory to leave buffer strips round the edge of the fields now and we don't maintain ours as well as we perhaps ought to. They argue that the hedge is a cornucopia of wildlife and habitat, which I agree, it is, but they've decided in their wisdom that if we leave a metre or more around the hedge then it will encourage wildlife out into the fields, which I would challenge because if you leave it, it just goes scrubby and the young partridge and stuff, you can see them struggling to get through it because it's just too dense. People walk round these strips (with their) dogs: there is no wildlife within 20 metres of the footpath because the dog has put all the birds up. We're obligated and trying to do our bit for nature and it doesn't work, which is very frustrating.

The Common Agricultural Policy all comes from Europe. It's so very complicated. I haven't got a complete handle on it and just as you think you've got a handle on it then all of a sudden they don't necessarily move the goal posts, they change the bloody pitch! Europe sends out guidelines and our government, DEFRA as it's now known, embellish what comes out as a guideline originally, and then Natural England and the rural agencies embellish a little more and all of a sudden we're saddled with the obligations. The single farm payment scheme, which is part of the Common Agricultural Policy, as it stands now, I've got a handbook that is about 3 inches thick!

Every acre of farmed land was eligible to join the scheme 4 or 5 years ago. To be eligible for payments we have to demonstrate that we're doing what they think is best to manage the environment. It's so complicated, it's impossible. As a farmer I find it very difficult to justify how we get paid. What I will say in the farmers' defences, for the last 3 years the single farm payment element in my accounts has been the difference between profit and loss. Had we not had the single farm element the farm would have lost money. With our 500 acres, we get about £35000 a year, paid in euros.

Government need to understand that food prices are going up and my profit is going down, so somewhere there's got to be balance. I hear business people talk about percentage return on assets; If you looked at our business exclusively through an accountant's eyes - the land base we've got and the machinery and stuff - it's a fraction of 1% return on your assets, which doesn't make sense. But it's the way of life, it's what we've always done.

Problems with the public

I don't like fencing. It's not as much of a problem now we've no livestock. One of the problems we have being on the urban fringe is people walking across crops where they just don't think. Occasionally I'll challenge or speak to them. Because it just looks like grass, they can't see that there's a problem at all. So we do have some wire on some of the fences but - barbed wire - I hate it. If we're patching up fencing or trying to keep things in or out, it seems to rip me to shreds every time we go near it.

In the summer because of what we do it's very dry and fiery we do get hedges on fire. We have lost 10 or 15 acres where kids have set fire to a bit and the fire's just run over it. 3½ tonnes of wheat to the acre at £150 per tonne, perhaps £600 per acre.

We have several public footpaths on the farm. I would say they are all fairly well used. And when people stick to the footpaths, that's absolutely fine, and when people walk with their dogs on the footpath, again, that's absolutely fine but they'll leave the dog off the lead and the dog will be running in and out of the crop, thinking it's great fun and they'll be throwing sticks for their dogs into the field and I'll pick up the said sticks with my combine when I go through and it has done damage before. I suppose the most daft thing I've had, a push bike, because, obviously when you're combining it's sort of 3 foot high and because you're working on such a growth you can't see what's going on and I've had bikes and things stuck in the combine. They don't like that!

Fly tipping is a problem and also joy riders and kids or stolen cars getting burnt out and people recklessly driving across the fields which is just such a sad thing to see.

We get less trouble now with just groups of kids playing in the fields than we've ever had: parents don't like their children going out of their sight - the days of going out at 10 o'clock in the morning and "We'll see you when it's dark" has gone. And also, the kids, the Play stations and the Wiis that they like, they have a different expectation of entertainment now.

Job satisfaction

Every morning when I wake up I appreciate the life that I have and I'm able to share with the people around me. There's nothing I really don't enjoy.

Harvest is a glorious time because it's nice weather and it's the culmination of your year's work but, equally, I like the planting because I know that once the farm's planted nature will do its thing and you're getting ready. It's almost never ending. Working with dad - I'm in my mid-40s, Dad's in his 70s and we still work together very closely. We both involve each other in the decisions that we're doing. We have a chat for a few moments every morning. We do row. I'd be lying if I said we didn't, but we don't bear grudges and I think that's the important thing. We go up like a firework, we go bang, both say our piece and then in the next breath move on. The most galling thing is dad is usually right! 99 times out of 100, experience has taught me that what he suggested is the way forward.

From left: John Hicklin and son, Edward.

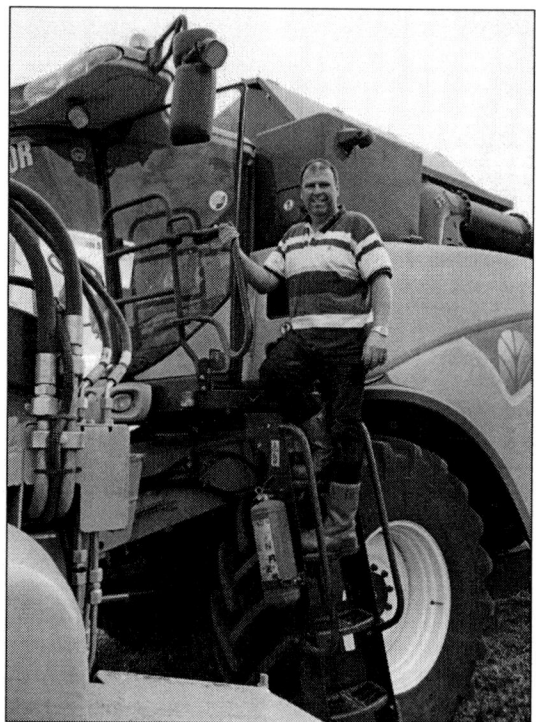

Ed Hicklin and New Holland Combine Harvester

ROLLS-ROYCE WORKER-NOW

Mark Tittley

Mark Tittley

Background and house in Chellaston

I was born at the City Hospital, Derby. The family connection with this area is strong. My father lived in Alexander Street as a boy and was evacuated (to Chellaston) on the outbreak of war to "The Field" on Sinfin Moor Lane.   He stayed there until Christmas during the "phoney war" and then went back home, but he was there for a long enough period to really like the area. When they bought their own house, my parents moved to Shelton Lock and I stayed there until I was first married. My father now lives in Chellaston.

I went to Shelton Lock Infants and Junior and then to Merrill Comprehensive School. I was Ward Councillor for Chellaston from 2004 to 2008, so I know the area fairly intimately.

(My house was once lived in by local artist, Cuthbert Gresley, famous for decorating china at Crown Derby). The garden was a field – we had it ploughed, it's that long. When I dug down I found that in some areas you could dig down no more than 6 inches. The reason was that there was a set of foundations for almost professional standard glasshouses. I am told by my own father, that Cuthbert grew his own vegetables for the "Travellers' Joy" while he worked at Crown Derby. So I guess that is the most tangible expression of Cuthbert living here, other than the fact that my wife is a good amateur artist and is carrying on the tradition of Cuthbert.

Mark's wife, Jill, outside their Derby Rd. house, which at
one time belonged to artist, Cuthbert Gresley.

Rolls-Royce in the family

(My father) started out at R-R in 1944 as a craft apprentice on the inspection section. They were all working flat out on the Merlin and Griffin engines that powered the Spitfire and the Lancaster. He is a Chartered Engineer like myself. In that sense I have carried on in the family tradition.

Starting work at Rolls-Royce

I think that most people who work at R-R recognise that if they are committed to it, it isn't just a job, it's a way of life. A lot of people may not articulate it as I am doing now but it's more than just a job, you are carrying on a dynasty really in terms of engineering quality and excellence. It is a privilege to work for the Company. I've worked there since 1978. I was 16, nearly 17. I think in the old Company there was a realisation that if your father worked there and was committed to the Company and the task, it stood you in good stead. I'm not sure that's true now.

I've always had, from the age of 14, a strong belief that collectively we are as good as the Society we produce and I saw engineering as a very honest way to earn an interesting living but moreover contributing to the gross national product of the country and the area we live in.

I started out as a craft apprentice. I was pleased to be accepted. At that time, it was a 3 year apprenticeship. My education other than on the job training consisted of ONC, HNC and then I did a degree part time with the Open University in Mechanical Engineering; so, while working, I was in part time education for some 13 years.

Various jobs at Rolls-Royce

I was not the most practical of people so, although I was doing well at the Technical College it was felt, mutually, a good idea if I went and worked in the laboratories as a technician. I worked in the Composite Labs. from 1979 onwards for a period of 5 years whilst I got my ONC. It was great fun because it made you grow up quickly. It led me into the Stress Office, material testing and making laboratory specimen pieces. The apprenticeship itself was very thorough and vigorous. You were put through your paces.

In 1989, I went into Product Support: I went into the Service Data Analysis Room which was looking at in-service data support and analysing the in-service record of the engines – how they were operating in service. That was extremely interesting.

Between 1991, after I graduated, and 2003, I went back into the Stress office. I started off as a junior technologist, progressed up the ranks and became a principal technologist about the year 2000. I was working exclusively on low-cycle fatigue in engines and life management of the product in-service.

There were several fellows in the stress office who could do The Times crossword within a half hour lunch break. You've got to be a bit smart to do that. You'd get people in there would go to work in bow ties; that sort of thing was quite the norm. There were a few characters around like that. I had a lot of admiration for their talent and knowledge.

One guy who had a high reputation in the business and lives locally is Arthur Shardlow, a metallurgist. He helped to evolve the material technologies that we employ today. It was just great to be able to work with a group of people who had been and were on the cusp of engineering advancement and technology.

Some would never use two words when one would do; people who made foolish comments weren't tolerated lightly. I became actively involved in the Union in about 1986 and except for the 2 years that I was in Product Support, I've always been involved in Trade Union activities. I became a senior rep. In 2003, when my predecessor retired, I ceased to be a practising engineer and I was elected to the position of Joint Chief Negotiator. That's the role I have been doing there since.

The company

R-R is the largest employer in Derby. The Company employs about 11/12,000 people; the other thing to be born in mind is that for every one job at R-R there are 3 jobs in the supply chain. Some of the supply chain is abroad but there is still a large content of it in the UK. Locally, there is something like a horseshoe that fans out from Derby and goes down and around and into the West Midlands. So that's an awful lot of jobs.

What we build, design and service at Derby, are the large by-pass engines, the Trent engines - the Trent 1000, 900 and 800. They are the successors to the RB211. They are 3 shaft engines, big fans at the front. The new one we are in the process of designing and certifying is the Trent XWB and that's a very significant engine. With some of these engines the casings are more or less touching the ground and coming up to the wing. They are very big - perhaps one and a half times the diameter of the original RB211, if not more.

The main aero engine design, manufacturing facilities and repair service are based on the Sinfin site now. When Nightingale Road was closing there was a new facility built on Wilmore Road which is effectively Nightingale Road moved to that facility.

One of the Roll- Royce Sinfin sites on Wilmore Rd.

Nightingale Road was a hundred years old and whilst the Marble Hall and all the rest of it on the front block have been kept, it was a facility that was becoming increasingly too expensive to run. The only facility that we still operate to the north of the ring road is Elton Road.

Roll- Royce Marble Hall, Nightingale Rd. Derby

The intention is to keep the Marble Hall. It is protected, so whatever else happens to the back of the facility it will be retained.

There is a fairly long period of gestation in terms of research and technology funding and then the basic design concept. Once it's been decided, a new engine will be built in about 3 – 4 years. During this period the new engine will be certified for use by the Civil Airworthiness Authority and the American equivalent, the Federal Airworthiness Authority.

What you are always trying to do is to make sure the design is at its lightest in terms of weight to enable it to operate in such a manner, delivering maximum power, which actually means you are running the engine at higher speeds and at higher temperature. So you are always expanding the boundaries on the material technology and the design technology - something that R-R is used to doing.

One of the things we have always been focused on is ensuring that in the high by-pass engines noise is maintained at a minimum.

(R-R's) complex turning, grinding and milling machines are vastly bigger than we used to have and procured from all over the world. They are complex machines, costing many, many thousands of pounds but obviously they are also capable of producing components to consistently reliable dimensions.

15 to 20 years ago there were three big players - Pratt & Whitney, G.E. (and) R-R was third. We are now second. R-R does very well because it is operating in four sectors but it is not physically the size they are. That's down to the quality of the product. It's down also to the technology, the advancement in technology and the commitment of the workforce in providing the product on time, reliably and to quality.

Because of the size of our order book, we are making sure we maintain a very large amount of work in Derby. So whilst R-R might have manufacturing facilities and design capability elsewhere there is no indication from the Company that it's going to do any less in Derby than it does now. Derby without R-R is not imaginable.

Above and below: views of Rolls-Royce works, Wilmore Rd. Sinfin.

The workforce

There are a lot of high skilled, high salary jobs relatively speaking in this area. We did a survey on the Council some 5 years ago which showed this. The average salary in Derby was £30,000 and at that time it was £25,000 in Nottingham. We have a lot of highly skilled, technical and manual workers working in Derby and relative to the retail or finance industry, the salaries are higher. I know 30 years ago and I think it is quite true now, it was said in the U.K. there are more graduates working at R-R in Derby, than anywhere else outside Oxford or Cambridge. Apprentices come from anywhere across the U.K. and if you look at the graduate recruitment level, we recruit not just in the U.K. but internationally.

Role as Works' Convenor

Although I am a Chartered Engineer, I am now the full-time Chief Negotiator, Convenor. I'm still a R-R employee, paid by R-R, but effectively I am a full-time staff convenor, for the R-R white collar staff, responsible ultimately for representing white collar staff, collectively, on pay terms, conditions and other collective agreements.

Along with a colleague, Simon Hemmings, we communicate with the members, write newsletters – one example on the discussions on pay. We link up and work with R-R Trade Union colleagues from all the UK sites and they stretch from Scotland down to the West Country. So, a typical day could be any of those issues – dealing with pay or terms and conditions, shift rates, potentially weekend working arrangements. No two days are the same.

We would argue as a union that a good work/life balance is essential. In reality people are committed to the Company and they do put in the hours at times when the business demand requires it. Our members are highly committed and the share price hasn't risen to the level it has just by people giving a normal 9 – 5 day.

Interest in politics

I have always been interested in politics, My role model, very old fashioned these days, is Harold Wilson. I joined the Labour Party because, whilst recognising that times change, I am more a traditional Labour man. I saw the value of having someone in that full time convenor's position involved in local politics.

The sad reflection for me, is that through successive Government industrial policy, since the late 70s, there has not been an emphasis placed on engineering being an essential backbone of our economy. There has been too much reliance placed on being a service industry economy which is a false dawn. Hence we have seen many companies across the U.K. go to the wall; that includes some very good machine tool manufacturers.

Becoming a councillor

I think it is just great to be able to represent people and their needs. One of the virtues that somebody brings with a trade union background is that they know how to represent people on big issues and individually. I think that's a great strength when you come to do the job as councillor.

(When I was Councillor for Chellaston 2004-2008), the main issue was people who were concerned about policing youths being disruptive on a Friday and Saturday night. That did result in us bringing extra police into the area and a Dispersal Order for a while. That's a bit of the stick but the carrot was we put some more youth provision in at the time.

We did get a weight restriction on the A514 – I will claim that one. The thing that did not come to fruition but looks as if it is (doing) now, was the building of the T12 road. Why didn't it reach fruition? Well, we were hit by the world recession. It was just co-incidental with when I lost office. Hopefully with the expansion of the new technology campus that is going to be built out on Wilmore Road - which will include very many high technology organisations - the T12 will now be built.

This year I had the privilege of being elected for Alvaston. I am chair of the Corporate Scrutiny and Climate Change Board. I am also chair of the Labour group of councillors. In my chairmanship of the Corporate Scrutiny Board, one of the prime things we are looking at is regeneration, re-skilling and job creation - high technology job creation. That's one of the prime focuses for the leader of the Council.

Work/life balance – with work and council duties

My working day usually starts about 6.15 in a morning, when I start to do some emails on the I pad perhaps. I come back about 5 o'clockish, if I haven't got meetings, and I'll probably do an hour or so of, emails, correspondence. On the evenings I have got meetings then it's fitting it in around meetings and you can be there until 8 o'clock at night or full Council meeting every 6 weeks, 9 o'clock at night. So, you do work long hours but then nobody asks you to be a councillor, it's something you have chosen to do yourself. I'm not unused to working long hours (particularly) when I was studying. Quite often as a young man I worked 16 hour days.

You've got to be quite fastidious in making sure to give space to yourself, your wife and family. (I try to do) no work on a Friday night other than the occasional Friday surgery. I might go out and do some leafleting for the Labour Party on a Sunday morning but I tend not to work on a Sunday otherwise. Saturday afternoons I'll take off. One of the great improvements I've seen is the technology with computers being very fast and efficient.

We've got a boat – we're keen narrow boaters - so we'll take the boat out at weekends even in the winter, which is good for the boat and for us. We keep it locally in South Derbyshire. You expend a bit of energy which you don't do when you are driving a desk all week. You think of Weston Cut - it's hardly far from where we are sitting now, but it can be a million miles away.

ROLLS-ROYCE WORKER

WARTIME

John Wain

Background – policeman's son

I was born in 1926 in Clay Cross in the Lockup in Market Street. At 3 months old I had to be operated on by the local doctor and the operation took place on the kitchen table. My mum, who was still recovering from a difficult birth, my own birth, wasn't up to holding me. Adie Dicken from next door, who to me was Auntie Adie, held me and the chloroform pad whilst the doctor operated on me and I have got the receipt for the operation to prove it.

My father was a young police constable at South Wingfield, Derbyshire. We lived right opposite to the entrance to Wingfield Manor. This collie called Bob, lived in a kennel outside. Dad was on duty at Alfreton and there was a bit of trouble at one of the pubs with a drunken miner. My dad left his dog Bob guarding the bike in a shop doorway with his cape over the handlebar. Unfortunately, he left his Lucas King of the Road oil lamp on and that set fire to the cape. Various people tried to get to the cape to get it off the handlebars but Bob wouldn't let anyone near it until my dad got back and of course, he had to buy a new police cape which was expensive.

We eventually moved to Shirebrook and we lived in a terrace. Shirebrook was a mining town. Dad had to go to the pithead on pay day so that the miners' wives could collect part of the men's wages - otherwise the miners wouldn't have got past the first pub on the way home. Whilst we were at Shirebrook the local dog-racing stadium/track was built and dad got a commendation for prosecuting a group of people who were wiping and spraying their dogs' backsides with turpentine to make them run faster.

He was transferred from Shirebrook to Ilkeston and we lived in a cottage by the side of the Erewash Canal. Ilkeston was an eye-opener for me. The policemen had to walk about in pairs, never allowed to walk alone particularly at night. There was a huge Irish contingent who had been left over from building the canal and also the Ironworks. They got jobs and just stayed there. There was always friction between the locals and them. The Market Place on a Saturday night, it was no place to be, but it was there I found out that somehow I was different to other kids. I overheard a father of one of the few friends that I'd got saying to his son, "What you playing with him for? He's Bobby Wain's lad. He'll shop you if you do owt".

Dad swam for the County and got medals, life-saving. He had spent hours and hours trying to teach me, so he was very disappointed in me that I couldn't swim. The water in the Erewash canal was warm but it was also a very rusty brown colour and with the help of the other kids we stripped off, not always starkers, but just to your underpants and within a short time I was swimming with the rest of them in what was known as 'Stanton Warms'. I went home looking rather like a Red Indian and my underwear a similar colour. My mum was very angry about it but my dad was more philosophical – he said at least he can swim now – so I got away with it.

By the following spring (1934) dad had been promoted to sergeant and we had moved to Alvaston, in the old village. The Police Station was almost opposite the church. There were 4 working farms within two or three hundred yards. I used to fetch the milk from a farm in a jug with a cloth over it, still warm, straight out of the cow.

I could walk over the road into the first field across the gravel pit field to the lodge gates at the bottom of Elvaston Lane. Then it was Oak Flatts and I was at the kennels at the Castle in no time. I loved roaming about all over there. You see, the policemen had a great big kennel with iron bars and had no option but to keep stray dogs for 7 days. At the end of the 7 days they were destroyed and my dad, having a car, would take them to the Fire Station in Bold Lane and they put a brass collar on them and electrocuted them there. My dad did not enjoy it one little bit. He didn't like destroying a fit dog or the time he had to spend doing it. So he had a word with Jack Clarke who was the head kennel man with the hounds at the Castle. "Oh bring them over here, sergeant, and I'll put them down for you," he said. "They will be done humanely and we'll use the meat to feed the hounds." Anyway, it became my Saturday morning job - walk the dog for his last walk over the fields, have it put down and walk back, miserable with a lead and an empty collar. And I didn't enjoy doing it.

Education

I had started school at Shirebrook at 5 years of age - a Model Village school - it was some sort of experiment in the provision of an up-to-date school with verandas round it. On sunny days kids sat out and did lessons outside and it was all very progressive. Before I had been at school very long I got TB of the glands in my neck. I was completely cured but instead of starting school at 5, I did not start until I was 6. I was doing well at Shirebrook, then we transferred to Ilkeston and at Ilkeston they put me in a class that was one year below my age group just to see how I would cope - apparently they did this to all itinerant families.

(When we moved to Alvaston) I went to the National Church of England School, Elvaston Lane, where the lads were taught separately to the girls - into a classroom devoted to all ages from 5 to 14. That would be 1934.

My parents transferred me to Brighton Road Boys School. 1939 came and the school was turned over to the issue of ration cards, gas masks etc and all the children had no education for months and months, but fortunately the Headmaster of the village school let me go back there (until) Brighton Road school opened up again in about 6 months' time and I went back. I left school at 14 and no qualifications. I could read, write, do sums, add up and take away, all the basics but nothing else.

Work at 14

The only thing I was determined not to have anything to do with was mining and of course, at Alvaston no pits or anything like that. Next door to the Police Station lived the manager of a gents outfitters, Salt Brothers, who had a departmental store then on London Road, at Crewton, not far from Alvaston Park, so I started in a department at Salt Bros and I hated it.

(In 1940 a bomb struck). I went to work on the following morning and Salt Brothers had ceased to exist – all the windows were blown out, glass everywhere, the stock was hung about all over the place. That was it – no job, no nothing. I was scouting around and somebody said Barlow & Taylor at Market Place in Derby wanted an apprentice in the soft furnishings department, rugs, carpets – there were fitted carpets in those days but they were made up from body carpet which was a yard wide and hand stitched together to form any size you wanted. Now I did enjoy this because I wasn't serving in the shop, I was doing things with carpets.

Rolls-Royce 1942

(Barlow and Taylor) employed a man whose job it was to go to houses and fit carpets and all manner of different things and I got to go with him in the van. He said, "You like working with your hands don't you?" I said, "Yes, I like using tools." He says, "If I was you, I would get yourself off to Nightingale Road. You're only just 16. If you had gone to Royces, your apprenticeship proper wouldn't have started until you were 16."

He knew who the apprentice supervisors (were), in a little office in the front building, the Marble Hall, at one side. So I went there and knocked on the door. I remember he said, "What's 50%?" and I said, "Half." "Right - when can you start?" And that was it. So I went home and told my mum and dad I had got the job at Royces.

It was May 1942. I reported to this Apprentice Office (and was sent to) the Training School at Normanton Road Technical College. I went on grinding machines etc for six months and I began to like it. The chap in charge of the Training School said. "They want somebody in No. 6 shop," which meant nothing at all to me. He said, "It's the Tool Room – good job, Tool Room."

They made a lot of the cutters they used on machine tools, lathe tools, special form tools for engine parts, jigs, fixtures to hold components in the Main Works. They sharpened all the cutting tools that the Main Works used and so you got a very thorough grounding in the bits and bobs that helped production and I lapped it up. I thoroughly enjoyed the variety. I really did. There was something new every day and the men that you worked with showed you how to do things. If they saw you struggling they'd help you and it was almost like a big happy family.

My first wage packet was 19/11d, then there were stoppages because you were encouraged to buy your own tools. They supplied practically all tools in the stores but you were expected to have your own rule, your own 0 to 1 micrometer, your own this, that and the other in your tool box. They ran a scheme whereby you could have these tools and you paid only pennies a week stopped out of your wages and you gradually built up quite a chest of nice tools.

The area's defences in wartime

(In Allenton) the War Memorial Village - that was all cornfields. Where the Blue Peter is now but (in Alvaston) was a wood yard, wheelwrights - Shermans. Baker Street came all the way across Harvey Road, because that wasn't there then, and joined Boulton Lane. All in my dad's area, and every gun emplacement, every ack-ack unit in there was the old man's responsibility. Where all those concrete and steel houses are in Boulton Lane -that was all fields - was a great big rocket battery. I don't think it was ever fired but it was huge. Elvaston Castle grounds had ack-ack units. In Swarkestone on Lowes Lane there was a decoy.

With the smoke units all round the streets we had terrible fogs. There were hordes of cyclists. Coming home was a monumental task in those fogs, particularly if the paraffin smokers were on. I remember going home in a very thick fog – you couldn't see across the street. I (once) set off on a Trent bus and we all finished up in the Mitre car park – everybody milling about in there, took no end of sorting out.

July 1942 - Luftwaffe raid on Rolls-Royce

I was there on the day. I had just started my apprenticeship in the Tool Room. You had to sign in - 5 minutes to 8 was clocking in time. Us youngsters used to belt up the flights of stairs, which were wrapped round the lift shaft. The older men rode on the lift. One morning we got to the top and I was just clocking in and rat-a-tat-tat -

machine gun fire! The glass roof of 6 Shop was shattered. Everyone was diving under cover. There was a chap who worked on a great big plough grinder; it only did extremely rough work. It had a massive table. He hadn't started anything up but the table was right out at one end and he dragged me with him underneath this table as I came through the doorway. There were some huge marking-out tables, half a dozen people could be round them, cast iron things on legs. People were scrambling underneath them. All hell let loose, then crump-crump, big loud noises but it was later on in the morning, that we found out that Central Stores, Hawthorn Street and everything had been bombed. No-one was hurt. There had been no air raid siren, no warnings at all.

I have read all the accounts and the strafing of 6 Shop is never ever mentioned. It was a glass roof to get the maximum daylight and there was a big area in the middle with machines all the way round it. To get light through to the floor underneath, where the reduction gears were assembled, there was this big hole - so all this glass cascaded down to the girls on the floor down below.

Rolls-Royce work in wartime

(Working) Mon, Tues, Wed, Thurs, Fri, Sat morning was standard – Sat. afternoon if they were desperate. There was an awful lot of Sunday working. Being an apprentice I wasn't particularly interested in overtime – I wanted to be out enjoying myself. But the blokes, there was a standing joke – "If they lock the bloody gates they would climb over to get in!" They used to hide work and bring it out last thing on Saturday and the foreman would say, "You'll come in and finish that tomorrow will you?"

There were no test beds to test engines on. Some special engines used to go to Hucknall for test but those that were produced in Nightingale Rd were tested in the yard, in sheds with flame traps which sometimes worked, sometimes didn't. You could be walking down No. 3 Yard and down towards the bottom end there would be yards of flames shooting out of this shed. How the people in Addison Rd slept, I don't know, because you had the drop forge on one side of the works thumping out great big reduction gear blanks at Hawthorne St – you not only heard it, you felt it!

Everything was produced in drop forges. I can remember going in there to take some stuff back to the Tool Room and they were belting out these things. The top and bottom dies that they were using - the top die would pick up the part and let it drop on the floor or something and this red hot wheel came from behind me and through my legs. Frightened me to death!

They didn't have beer during the war but they had buckets of barley water and stuff like that, because the heat in there was something to believe. Before the war they had beer from the Nightingale, the pub at the bottom.

Women workers at Rolls-Royce

In Number 1 Shop and all the production shops a fantastic number of women worked on milling machines, lathes – you name it, they did it. The bulk of them went (after the war). They just got intensive training on a particular thing - perhaps on a drilling machine - they never did anything else. They would just drill holes in a particular component; they put this component into the shuttle or whatever it was, put the latch down, took out, put another one in – that was it - so it was very semi-skilled. Some girls got scalped - got their hair caught in the spindles. They had to wear snoods and caps to keep their hair out. There was a womans' inspection department who inspected nuts, bolts and washers. All they were doing was screwing a screw into a gauge to see if it wobbled - those were the sort of jobs. Now if you had put a bloke on doing that he would have been screaming at the end of the week. They never got bored; they could do that job and think about all manner of other things at the same time.

They were the sort of girls you would meet in shops, in fact, possibly better than the shop girls you get now. Some of them were quite intelligent. There was one I remember, had a marvellous singing voice. She'd sing along with 'Workers Playtime' but she was marvellous. She sort of mothered me a little bit.

The canteen

The canteen in Nightingale Rd was right opposite the Marble Hall – a huge canteen with a stage, everything - absolutely fantastic. Shows were put on there – at dinner time for the day workers and suppertime for the night workers. Ever so well-known people came to entertain us. There was 'Music while you Work' all the time.

The grub was really good - the puddings and things like that. They must have been special rations for factory workers and they were subsidised of course, ever so cheap. I started off taking sandwiches but it wasn't long before I abandoned sandwiches. You could have a main meal and a pudding and sometimes, being a youngster, I'd skip the main meal and have 3 puddings. They were really good.

You had to wear your badge all the time. Everybody had to pass through a little gate to pass the watchman. If you hadn't got your badge on they wouldn't let you in. There were two very fussy foremen, very pretentious, one was Cable but he insisted, "My name is not Cable – it's Ca-_bell_." The other one had forgotten his badge. He presented himself at the gate, and said, "My name's Jack Swan" - or something like that - and the gateman said, "Yes and my bloody name was Donald Duck – hoppit!" And he wouldn't let him in – he had to go home and get his badge and come back. They were very strict on that.

VE Day (Victory in Europe)

I could not remember at any time not knowing that we would win, that we would be alright, we would get through all this. I suspect my mum and dad were a little more apprehensive but I cannot ever remember being down beat. VE Day - I can remember that. I was on nights. They announced it over the tannoy system. Everybody downed tools; they went berserk. There was patriotic songs – everybody was singing their heads off. They seized all these little 3 wheeler Lister trucks and they were belting round the yard. In the finish they let us all go home to get rid of us because it was getting a bit out of hand.

Nightingale Rd during wartime. The Marble Hall on the left.

Working on Merlin engines during the 40s

Called up 1946

I always thought I was called up (to do) National Service but there was a big call up prior to them sorting out National Service and I was one of those. I was told they wanted to try and avoid what happened after the 1st World War when all the troops came home and there was massive unemployment. So anyone who was nearing the end of their apprenticeship was called up - those coming home (had) their jobs for 2 years.

I was called up in May 1946. I got my movement pass and arrived at Derby station (where) there was this crowd of lads with little suitcases and worried looks on their faces - all in suits waiting for the train for Warwick. We were all people from engineering firms - Royces, Qualcast, Midland Railway. We got on this train, got to Warwick and then from Warwick we went to Budbrook Barracks which was the Leicestershire Regiment - just outside Warwick. It was there we had our initial training – marching, mucking about and injections and I had my first eye opener about how many people there were who couldn't read or write.

I wanted to go in either the Engineers or REME. They asked you if you could read engineering drawings, work to a drawing or work to instructions and I came through all that with flying colours. When I got to the man – "Ah yes, your grandfather was a police officer, your uncle, your great uncle, your grandfather's brother was a Derbyshire police officer?" "Yes, sir" "You've got an uncle who is a police officer?" "Yes, sir." "Right, well the Military Police are being reformed as a voluntary organisation and there are no conscripts into the Military Police, they are all volunteers now. How do you feel about volunteering for the Military Police?" "No thank you, sir." "Why not?" "Well, they have got a terrible reputation, nobody likes them." "Well," he said, "there is the Pioneer Corps or the Catering Corps." I thought I don't want to do two years of spud bashing. So I opted for the Military Police.

Training in the Military Police

The three months training was great, except that they were determined to ill-treat you until you turned into the swine you didn't want to become. It was guards' type training from a square bashing point of view, the discipline was horrendous but the classroom work was great, I really enjoyed that. We had sten gun practice – one bloke got shot because they would run away with you; there were single or multiple shots - put it on single shot and it still shot. They were terrible things. We had .45 Webley pistols. The weight on those triggers was tremendous. By the time you had outstretched (your arm), when it fired there were bullets going all over the place. Definitely none at the target!

You had leather equipment, a leather Sam Brown (belt), leather holster, leather bullet pouch, which had to shine at all times. Your boots you could see your face in them - they were hobnail boots and steel shoes at the back, like little horseshoes. If you were marching on say a pavement with slabs that had any incline, you had difficulty keeping on your feet. You didn't wear battledress you wore box collar like a monkey suit they called them and I didn't like that at all.

Posting to Germany 1946

I read that they wanted volunteers for BAOR. "Where's BAOR?" "British Army on the Rhine." "That'll do me. I'm going." So I put my name down and off I went. I sailed from Hull. Got to Cuxhaven very late at night, and they shoved you into this building.

There were straw palliasses and bunks and your first job was to find enough slats to make a bed out of. The frame was there but the slats had got flung all over the place.

In the morning I went to another selection office and this officer said, "Ah yes, you are the police sergeant's son." - They knew more about me than I knew myself! I said, "Yes, sir." "Right, where do you want to go?" I said, "I don't know. Germany, wherever." "Well," he said, "you've got some experience of boats haven't you?" I said, "No, not really, I've just had a sailing dinghy on the Trent at Weston Cliff," which meant nothing to him. It was only a home- made sailing dinghy nothing posh. "Well" he said, "you know how to behave on water?" "Yes" and "You can swim?" "Yes, sir." "Right," he says, "how do you feel about joining the Military Police Motorboat Patrol in Hamburg docks?"

John Wain on his 21st birthday 1947, Hamburg.

John Wain and "Scouse"Feb 1947

Cuxhaven is at the mouth of the Elbe. I knew that Hamburg was a way up the Elbe and I thought, "That's not too far - if I go to Hamburg I'm not too far away from home for going on leave." So I said, "Yes, I think I would like that, sir." I got on a train with my movement pass – German trains then were wooden seats, laths and very uncomfortable. You could have got off and walked it in places, the track was so bad and the speed was so restricted. I looked out of the windows, both sides, and everywhere along that track was pockmarked with bomb holes. It's almost all country on the way to Hamburg. There was hardly 200 yards without some sort of explosion had occurred.

Hamburg

As I got nearer to Hamburg all you could see was church towers, the odd tall chimney, everywhere else was just rubble and flat. I had seen a bit of the damage in London, I knew about Coventry being flattened – and I'd seen pictures - but I'd never, ever witnessed anything like Hamburg was. It was 75% flat – everywhere you went you drove through canyons of rubble where they had cleared the road and just piled it up on either side.

(I was billeted in) this gorgeous private house in a leaf-lined street, something like Friargate , with really nice houses, all intact, no damage at all. For the first time in my army career I slept in a nice single bed with snowy white sheets and blankets. The toilet was out of this world, never seen a toilet like it. There were all manner of innovations they may have had in posh hotels in London but not in houses I knew.

There were just a few of us. In the cellar there was a storekeeper. He issued all the kit and was the general collector of info and knowledge. He was older than the rest of us by a long chalk. We had a cobbler who was down there with him who was actually a shoemaker. He made me a pair of shoes. We had 2 waitresses and a lady who did the washing. A building on the opposite side of the street was our mess; that was rather like a small version of our Church Hall. In there we had a brilliant cook, and he had a helper. All of these we paid for, because they weren't official – well we fed them - we paid for them with coffee, cigarettes or anything we could get our hands on and they were very grateful.

We had a little HQ in the docks. If it was a gorgeous day we could climb on the boat and please ourselves largely to where we went. We just roamed about looking for thieves and robbers. We used to go onto the lakes which were connected to the canal system that went into the Russian Zone. Refugees on boats were trying to come down. We used to stop those and search them and if we found anybody who shouldn't have been there or contraband or anything we handed it over to the town provos, the military police.

The German population were having a real rough time. People collapsed in the street and if they did, anyone on their feet would immediately strip them of their clothes. They fought each other. Very occasionally, not every day, part of a day maybe, the electricity would be on and the trams running and they pulled each other off - the younger element pulled the older element - slung them off the tram so they could get on. They'd ride on the buffers, they'd ride everywhere clinging onto the running boards at the sides.

All the trees went at the side of the road. There were no stray dogs or cats, they all got eaten. One of our jobs in the docks was trying to prevent them jumping off a bridge onto a moving train that had got coal on it, filling a sack and then chucking the sack off with coal in and jumping off after it. As we walked about, the odd lump of stone or brick would be dropped off a bridge near to you.

One of the waitresses who looked after us was a middle aged woman – I'm 20 by this time, she'd be in her 30s – her husband was still in Russia as a POW. I found her in tears – I'd been for a late night cup of cocoa and sandwich, and she was still there and shouldn't have been. I said, "You still here Inger, why haven't you gone home?" "I'm frightened, I daren't go home. They are robbing people, there's all manner of nasty things happening." Practically everybody spoke English and I said, "Well look,

Hamburg after the war

I'll walk you home." So I am walking her down the street. We've left our opulent villas behind and we're into the rubble now and I'm waiting for some flat or dwelling to appear and she says, "It's here." And she pointed to the steps going down into a cellar. All there was on top was rubble – a demolished building's cellar steps and doorway that was half off its hinges. I took her down there and she invited me in. She'd got an electric light bulb and a boiling ring and they were both permanently on. Somebody had driven nails into a cable that was still live and attached bulldog clips to these 2 spikes. She left them on permanently because she was frightened to use the clips to (turn them off). She wasn't paying for it, there was no meter. That's how she lived and that's how a lot of them lived. If there was a spare bit of ground, like a garden or an allotment and they could get a barrow, they could have as many bricks as they liked to clear off the bomb site and they could build themselves a hovel with a flat roof out of anything they could scrounge, no mortar, just brick on brick, tied together and bonded. No end of them were living like that. So, they really did suffer.

115

German Prisoners of War return from Russia 1948

Our little group were sent for by the Commanding Officer and he said, "I've called you together because I'm sending you on a special mission but I've got to swear you to secrecy, you mustn't talk about it, you mustn't write letters home. If you've got cameras you are not allowed to take them. You're going to Altona Station and you're going to meet the very first POWs that Russia has reluctantly released. When you get there, there will be International Red Cross people, but there will only be you, no Germans allowed, even the engine driver is going to be a British soldier." I knew where Altona Station was - a bit like Friargate, but a dead end – it didn't carry on anywhere. You went to Altona and you went the same way out again.

So we duly arrived at Altona station and we are on the platform. It's so little used there are weeds growing in the track – couldn't have been in a better place. Eventually this train appears, coming in backwards - coaches came in first, the engine was at the far end. I think there were 4 coaches. So we are there agog waiting for the windows and the doors to be opened, heads to appear and nothing happened at all. Nothing. So we stood there like idiots for what seemed ever such a long while, but it could only be about 5 minutes, if that. Eventually we walked all the way down the train looking in the windows and there were these piles of rags with heads on, just sat there.

We got on the train and it smelt awful, it was terrible, the stink and we said, "Righto, raus, raus" which is, "Out – get out". It's not the word you should use but it's the only one we did know. Nothing happened at all so eventually I grabbed hold of one and made him stand up. He shuffled, I got him down on the platform and there he stood. A mate of mine brings another one out and stands him and eventually we've not got them all out but we've got a considerable number out - enough for them to be taken to buses. They were going to take them to a transit camp prior to them going home and they just stood there. "Righto – off you go!" No movement at all. Somebody had to grab hold of the first one and take him but we made him hold the hand of the next one and they walked along like a row of elephants, the trunks holding each other's tails. It was the saddest sight I have ever seen, terrible it was and anyway they were all taken to hospital and instead of going home they spent months in hospital.

Like skeletons they were, emaciated. They were dressed in remnants of uniform; some had got a forage type cap on still with the army badge - they have like little buttons of army badges on forage caps. Others had got remnants of footwear on, others had just got rags bound round their feet – terrible. Their hands were claw like – you thought if you gripped them too hard you'd break them and they didn't walk they shuffled. I don't know what unit or anything about them whether they had been a particular SS unit or something like that and they'd been meted special bad treatment or not I don't know, but if all Russian prisoners of war were like that then ...

After it was all over and the train had gone, we got back and the APM was there - the Assistant Provo Marshall - got us all in again. He was unaware to begin with, what we were going to meet, but they informed him. We were sworn in again with dire consequences. If the press had got hold of it, if there had been any pictures or publicity, Russia would never have sent any more home.   These people were those that had starved the Russians at Stalingrad. The hatred the Russians had for the Germans had to be seen to be believed. I never talked about it even when I was demobbed and I came home.   I never talked about it for ages and ages.

Jewish settlers come to Hamburg1948

The state of Israel was formed (1948) and the traditional hatred of the Germans for the Jews really surfaced again. The Jews had been brought back from the ship they were trying to get to Israel on. This rust bucket that they were on was in the Mediterranean. It was so low in the water - they were sleeping in shifts. They were supposed to have taken all their own food and water with them and that had all run out.   Everyone was selling everything they had got, to get on these boats. Unscrupulous agents were just robbing them blind, putting them on boats; some of them never got anywhere near Israel.

The Navy intercepted them and 3 little, tiny cruise liners from England were hurriedly sent out and it took 3 of them to load all this lot on to. They promised these people that they would continue their journey and in the night they turned round and the next thing they knew they were passing Gibraltar in the wrong direction and so they rioted on the ship. They tried to take the ships over.   They managed to get their hands on axes from the ship. They got scissors and they split the scissors up so they had got 2 daggers.

When they got to Hamburg, naval ships brought them up the Elbe under escort. When they got them into the docks they didn't let them come to the dock side they kept them out on dolphins - huge telegraph pole-like structures out in the fairway that ships were tied up to waiting their turn to dock. Complete clampdown, all leave stopped, everything.   All troops confined to barracks. Nobody could get into Hamburg.

(Germans) were trying to get into the docks because they had heard (about the Jews' arrival). I was at one of the gates to begin with. I thought there was every German in Hamburg on the opposite side of these gates and there's me and an interpreter, a German, quaking in his boots and I've got my revolver out and I thought when they break through those gates, they're just going to run over me. They'd have run riot if they had got in. I managed to get through on the phone and reinforcements came, not military police but troops came to control these gates and keep them back.

Eventually they brought one ship in and the gang planks were put up and they just refused to get off. The Sherwood Foresters were employed to unload them. I went back and was earmarked to a 3 ton truck ready to escort the troublemakers in wagons with handcuffs to Police Stations and anywhere else where they could be locked up. Of course there weren't many of us. It is very difficult coming down a gangway on a ship. It was taking one at each leg and one at each arm to try and carry them physically off the boat and they are struggling like 'Hee-Haws'. They brought these scissors and they were having a go at people.   One of them knocked my hat off and got hold of my hair at the front and for years afterwards if the wind ever got in to my hair and lifted it I could feel what he had done to my hair.

Anyway, the first boat was unloaded and they were going back to the displaced persons' camp that was still there, that they had originally been housed in. Many were young, not many were old people. They were put onto these coaches that had been specially stripped of anything that could be used as implements. Each coach had several great big vacuum flasks of soup and baskets of bread and stuff like that already put in for them. They had no sooner filled the first coaches when they used these flasks as battering rams to burst the tack welding off the mesh on the windows.

They forced the locked doors open and they were outside on the running boards on both sides.   They climbed onto the roof, I don't know why but none of them tried to jump off and run away. Possibly they realised the docks was ringed, no way could they get out of the docks.   Anyway, the engine driver, a German, drove straight under a loading gauge as he had got to do and wiped all those on the roof off. Most of them were killed and a bit further along when they got out of the docks (there was) a train coming the other way and they opened the doors and held them open with their feet and scraped a lot of those off that were on the outside, on the running board.

War criminals executed

I think that was a one-off incident, after that it got better. So gradually they were all back inside their displaced person camp. But the nasty part was the proper court where real Nazis were tried and they were taken to Hamlin where the Pied Piper came from. Pierrepoint used to come over from England and they had a choice – they could either be hung or the odd one elected to be shot. I didn't have anything to do with the execution, I accompanied them there. You sat in like a Black Maria with them and it wasn't in compartments, it was like an ambulance, blacked out window, seats along the side.   There were 2 in the one I escorted.   Sat with them and they were gibbering because they knew they were going to be executed but I only ever did it once. I wriggled out of it after that.

Marriage, de-mob and back to Royce's, 1948

I had to ask the C.O. for his permission to get married and Alma had to get her permission as well even though she was getting demobbed. They gave me a day extra for my honeymoon and I had to pay for that by collecting a prisoner AWOL in Harwich. I had to escort him all the way to Germany, but he carried my suitcase!

John went back to Royce's where he was upgraded to Inspector and then Machine Planner and in 1954 was promoted to Instructor in the Machine Training School. He left Royce's in 1959 to take an appointment as Assistant Lecturer at Derby Technical College Training School, where he had started his career in 1942.

PHARMACIST

David Railton

CHELLASTON PHARMACY 1992 – 2008

Background: childhood in Yorkshire and South Africa

I was born in 1966. My parents lived in Hull at the time. Mum died when I was 2. Dad remarried and when I was 5 we went to South Africa with Dad's business – for 13 years, until I was 18. So I did all my schooling there.

Only in retrospect do I realise what we experienced – at the time it seemed normal. We used to have regular practices for terrorist attacks - they'd ring a special bell and we'd get under our desks or you'd all have to go out in to the playground because they were practising for bomb scares and things like that. It was just routine. We were part of the ex-pat community. I never felt myself as part of the apartheid culture. As English people we were victims of a sort of cultural apartheid: we were British, rednecks, foreigners. We didn't have live-in servants or people to mow the lawns. We did that ourselves.

I matriculated in South Africa and went to Witwatersrand University in Johannesburg for one year to do pharmacy. I'd originally applied to do medicine, but didn't get the grades I needed. The fall-back was pharmacy. In 1984, after 13 years, we decided to come home because the South African government wanted everyone to do National Service, give up your British passport and stop dual citizenship.

Training as a pharmacist

I went to Bradford University to study pharmacy in 1985 – a 3 year degree course, then a year post-graduate work as a student before you can register with the Pharmaceutical Society – so it's 4 years before you qualify. Bradford was the only place at the time which offered a sandwich course. You did two 6 month periods in industry, hospital, community and that qualified as your pre-registration year.

It's now a 4 year course plus pre-registration which makes it 5 years in total. That reflects the changing nature of pharmacy. It's much more clinical- based now, more practical training about how to communicate with people. When I did it, it was much more science - based. Next to medicine it is probably the heaviest workload. We worked 9 'til 5 every day- mornings was all lectures, afternoons were practicals. If you don't turn up you don't pass.

I got a first class degree and registered in '89 - I worked hard. When I applied for a job there was almost zero unemployment (in pharmacy) so you walked away from your degree ceremony into a job.

First job – Derby City Hospital

My first job was at Derby. I wanted to come here because you could do a clinical pharmacy post-graduate diploma as part of your work on a fixed two-year contract. I was Resident Pharmacist – we lived on the premises and provided an out-of-hours service. I was on call one night a week each and one weekend in five. There were 5 of us on a rota. You carried a bleep and were called out all hours to provide a pharmacy service through the night – it was an experience!

We carried a crash–bleep so when someone has a heart attack in hospital, they call a crash team and you turn up with a bag of specialist drugs to help the cardiac team. I have memories of hurtling across the car park at three in the morning, with a black bag and white coat flapping to attend cardiac arrests. That was the first time I saw someone pass away and saw a dead body.

(I then) applied as a relief pharmacist at Burrows and Close in Nottingham. I knew the pharmacy aspect of it but it's using the cash register, ordering stuff, interacting with customers. It's different to interacting with patients in a bed.

Chellaston Peak Pharmacy

Mr Raynes retired in 1991 (from Chellaston Pharmacy) and a group called Peak Pharmacy bought it. I got the job – I started on 7th Sept. 1992. When I got there it had a nice village pharmacy kind of feel. The shop closed for lunch, it was half day on a Wednesday – the days were gentle, you were never so quiet you were bored, but you were never so busy that you didn't know where your next toilet break was coming from, which is how it ended up! I was the only pharmacist.

The pharmacy changed an awful lot when I was there. When I first went Mr Raynes' old shop was half the size. Joan Brown (the shop next door) sold up and the shop was expanded. Initially it was quite a gentle business, but by the time I left it was non-stop. I was getting there 15 minutes early, leaving half an hour late, not stopping (work) all day – due to population rise, more doctors and the NHS expecting more of you. We went from 3,000 prescriptions a month to about 10,000.

You're doing a prescription every one to two minutes - a lot of work. There was one pharmacist, a dispenser and one shop assistant.

It's a funny situation in a pharmacy: people walk in, hand you their prescriptions. They see the shop's empty – they don't see that 6 people have just dropped a prescription off and said, "I'll come back in a second," "I'm just going to post a letter". The chap's stood there waiting, thinking, "All I've got is a tube of cream, what's he got to do?" There was pressure and stress like that. There's a lot of accuracy involved and you need to get it right; you've got to have attention to detail and you have to keep your wits about you and know your customers.

One of the benefits of Chellaston is by the time I finished, we had some 12,000 patients on the books and some three quarters of them I would recognise, know their names and know their prescriptions. You need to know them because when you get a prescription you need to know whether it's appropriate or not.

Part of the pharmacist's role is a sort of gate-keeper, a kind of safety net for the doctors – less so in days when everything is done on computer. The computer system will tell the doctor the drug is not appropriate with a medicine. When they were handwriting prescriptions, they wouldn't necessarily know. But even with computers, it's still beholden on the pharmacist to check with a doctor.

I felt the sharp end of a doctor's tongue on more than one occasion: "That's what I want, that's what I'll get!" In the end you have to go with the doctor's clinical judgement. Often they were grateful for our interaction and help. It's more an equal footing relationship now, less so in the past. New doctors are more used to working with pharmacists.

I can only think of one occasion where I gave out the wrong strength of something. The patient took it for a month before the next prescription. We realised then, we'd given him the wrong strength, a higher strength. I remember feeling pretty lousy that it had happened, grateful he was all right. Fortunately it had no effect on him, in fact he felt better on the higher strength and he was going to ask the doctor if he could have them – an anti-depressant!

Prescription drugs – costs etc

There are thousands upon thousands of drugs - maybe 20 or 30 thousand. Over my 16 years (in Chellaston) you would see trends in types of drugs: a lot of anti-depressants – amazing number. They can be expensive – it varies from pence to tens of pounds per month.

The companies that produce the drugs, do all the testing etc, get a patent by right for something like 16 years, in which they can be the sole producers of that as branded medicines, for instance in the anti-depressant line, Prozac. They get a licence to allow them to recoup some of the costs of doing the clinical trials.

Say the Prozac cost is £15, once Prozac's rights are finished, any company can produce it and they don't have to go through the process of trials and they produce a generic brand called Fluoxetine which is the name of the ingredient and they will be selling that for £5. So once the rights have ended, the cost to the NHS goes down.

Statins is the other one that we noticed. Simvastatin, when it first came out, you'd be talking £30 a box to last a month. When the government were looking at lowering cholesterol levels, they did a deal with companies and said if you'll lower the price of these drugs, we'll promote their use in lowering cholesterol. The price went down from £30 to £4.80. Because they reduced the cost, more people were able to get them, so they changed the targets for cholesterol to much stricter levels which meant that more people fell into the treatment bracket, which meant more was prescribed – so the use of statins went up loads.

There's a lot of cheaper drugs. An average cost of a prescription works out - last time I was there - at something like £10.50, each prescription item. Aspirins (are) probably less than one pence each - very cheap and very cost-effective. When you think of a bottle of aspirin – 100 aspirins cost £1 – it shows you what the cost of the higher end things is that's pushing that average up.

Some of the older anti-depressants, are again only pence each - so still cost-effective. You think of antibiotics as being wildly expensive but the older antibiotics, Amoxicillins, Trimithoprims and things like that – a course is only going to cost you one or two pounds. Things like inhalers, steroid inhaler - the Ventolins are £2; whereas the blue inhalers are £20, so if you're getting two of those on a prescription that's £44 for a month's inhalers.

The rarer drugs are used in hospitals. Hospital budgets are different from community budgets. One patient could have maybe £10,000 worth of drugs per year. Community drugs are more standard. One of the rarer and more expensive drugs would be Eprex, which is Erythropoietin given to kidney patients to boost their red blood cell level, because when they have dialysis their red blood count drops. We'd occasionally get a dialysis patient for Eprex, which needs to be stored in the fridge and cost £500 for a box of 5 injections. That would be special delivery, brought in a refrigerated lorry - over a year £6000 maybe. Transplant patients would have drugs that help stop rejection. I remember once throwing away £20,000 worth of injections that were no longer needed - £90 an injection and we had hundreds of the things to throw away!

Often when patients die, and when treatment changes, you get back the old drugs to dispose of. They can't be re-used as you can't guarantee quality any more. They're put in bins and taken away for incineration. Absolute fortunes! Campaigns are run all the time that doctors should only prescribe 28 days at a time, "Take the tablets you've got", "Finish your antibiotics" "Don't get tablets you don't need". But with the repeat prescription system, people, particularly older or confused people, think if it's on their list they must order it and then they're not taking them! They haven't taken last month's and they are getting a new pack. We just throw them away.

I'm sure people who have benefitted from those drugs wouldn't begrudge spending that money. People may balk at the cost of treating drug addicts who are perceived to have brought it on themselves, people wanting cosmetic surgery, or people being treated for smoking-related illnesses. Cancer is more emotive; people will front up and accept that, will accept treating kidney transplants.

The NHS is far stricter and more careful than it used to be. Before my time - speak to Jim Raynes - the doctor could prescribe anything on the NHS, quite literally. If they put a tin of Heinz beans on the prescription, the pharmacist would provide beans! A bottle of Guinness, food, clothing, exercise - anything!

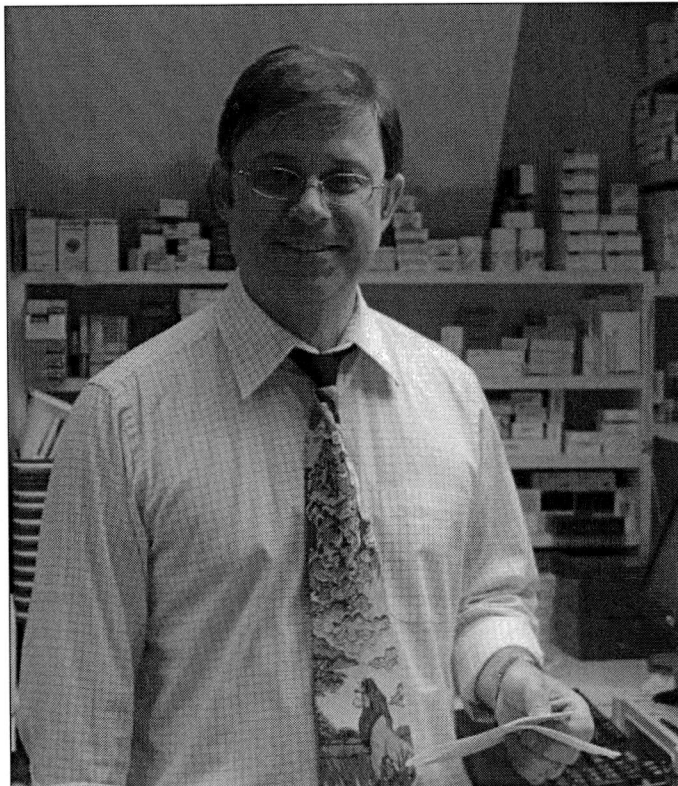

David Railton in Chellaston Peak Pharmacy

Before I started pharmacy they introduced the "Black List" – things that couldn't be prescribed. There was an allowable list of prescribed medicines and that's reviewed all the time. It's much more closely policed than it used to be so some of the high-end expensive things, the NHS thinks, "This isn't value for money. We are not going to reimburse for it," - this is what NICE does (National Institute for Clinical Excellence). Overall the NHS gets value for money, but it's a bottomless pit. It's not just the cost of the medicines, it's the cost of the equipment, treatments; as new things are produced, the cost goes up and up.

Placebos

In the days before I started, the doctor could ask for sugar tablets and ask the pharmacist to label it as "The tablet" so the patient wouldn't know what they were getting. It got to the point where you weren't allowed to prescribe a placebo because of legal considerations. Now you have to put on what the tablet is. The placebo effect is that the patient thinks they're getting an active medicine, but they're not. Hoodwinking the patient isn't allowed to go on any more. The only time you'll get that is in a randomised trial where some people will get the active medicine and some will get the sugar tablets. A doctor can't prescribe a placebo; the best they can do is give you a Paracetamol tablet and say "That's going to do the trick". Sometimes antibiotics are given on that basis: the doctor knows what you've got is a virus but if it makes you feel better, will prescribe antibiotics – less so now, because there is quite a bit of awareness about inappropriate prescribing of antibiotics, but at one time they'd have done just that – so the patient goes away happy.

Old fashioned remedies, leeches

In the early days – I started in 1991 - in hospitals, (we mixed) eye-drops, injections, suppositories, emulsions etc. Even in the community pharmacy we did make some things, mix simple things together, liquids, ointments, the odd powder; mainly mixtures – cough medicines and tonics, very old fashioned remedies some of the doctors like to prescribe. As time went by, for any manufacturing you had to have a manufacturing licence - so now it is done by manufacturers.

One or two doctors would prescribe some of the older things. There wasn't a modern equivalent for Mist. Gent. Alk - a tonic that is supposed to help stimulate your appetite. Whether it worked or not is questionable, but it wouldn't do any harm. There is a place for placebos in medicine. Because it's an old fashioned medicine, there aren't any clinical trials which prove efficacy. That doesn't mean it doesn't work. The placebo effect plays a part: and to think it's doing them good, well it is doing them good – as long as they feel better, it's worked.

They (use leeches) in hospitals, particularly if you've had a finger or an arm sewn back on to keep the blood flow going. When I started out at the Derby City Hospital one of my co-pharmacists at the DRI, who I'd only met once, rang and pretended to be a doctor, on Ward 32, wanting the leeches please. I'd only been there two or three weeks. I didn't know where the leeches were, so I rang my 2nd on call. She said, "Oh, they're in the cupboard at the bottom of the pharmacy." The cupboard was just a broom cupboard –there weren't any leeches at that time, they were just having me on!

 It was just my first night on call - just pulling my leg a little bit. 10 years further on, medical leeches were back in vogue again, so if someone asked for the leeches now, you could provide them.

Cough medicines

A lot of medicines aren't cures, they are symptom relief. Things will go away in a week or two, but in our modern world people don't want to live with the pain. People in the past would have put a piece of brown paper and vinegar on it and got on. Because of the modern mind set people aren't prepared to do that, they want to feel better now. A lot of over-the-counter remedies are symptom relief, they don't cure it.

There are different kinds (of cough medicine) and I wouldn't blanket them as ineffective. They do have an effect on a dry cough. When a cough is bothersome you can get things that stop you wanting to cough and will help to some extent. They won't cure it but it will relieve the symptoms while your body cures itself.

The main problem is a chesty cough: there is no real benefit from taking expectorants – they don't necessarily work. You're probably as well to drink plenty of fluids because all an expectorant does is loosen up the chest so you can cough it up. Whether they work or not is questionable. But people wanted something. I'd suggest sometimes take it with some warm water – maybe the warm water does the trick.

Non–prescription work

The profitability to pharmacies comes more from the sale of medicines over the counter and the sale of other things than from prescription work. For prescription work you get paid a price per prescription and it's the same no matter what's on it, so it's of no value to the pharmacist to have higher priced drugs on it because you don't make anything on it, you get paid piece-work. It ranges depending on how many items you do over the course of a month. For instance for the first 10,000 you do, you get paid 80p an item, the second 10,000 you get 60p an item – it's a sort of scale like that. So the more you do, the more you get but it doesn't depend on what's on the prescription.

These days, things have shifted much more towards the clinical side of it. Medicine-use reviews, smoking cessation clinics, anti-coagulation monitoring and pregnancy testing - they're added value to the pharmacist. You get paid for providing those services each time you provide them. So there is more value in doing things like that, being proactive and more involved in patient care than doing the piece work of prescriptions.

Customers

I can think of a few occasions when I've told someone to stop being silly and get on with it, kind of thing - fussing over medicines etc. One situation really got on my nerves – the demand for a specific brand of a tablet over a generic, the generic being the low cost version - and people wanting a specific pack, with specific colour print on the tinfoil. A number were as fussy as that –"If it doesn't have the black writing on it, it doesn't work like the one with the red writing!"

People would come in and ask for advice on whatever it was that was the matter with them. You make a recommendation and they choose to take it or not. When I first went in to the pharmacy it would be a case of me peering over the counter and having a look. Towards the end of my time, most pharmacies have a private consultation area and some larger than others – rooms with sinks and the full works. I've had people come in and take their shoes and socks off or drop their trousers – "Look at this rash" – not an examination as the doctor would give you.

A lot of things are cases where you say you need to see your doctor, sooner rather than later. You would say "If you are still bothered by it, still concerned, go and show it to your GP." You would get other things where you would insist someone goes to a GP. If a child comes in with impetigo you say, "Oh no, that's not a cold sore, that's impetigo. Go to your doctor, you need antibiotics." We often did that.

In any walk of life there are always those "heart-sink" people; but your professionalism means that you deal with them, and they get extended the same courtesy that everyone else does. Some people come in and the staff disappear and you're left – you have to deal with it. There are people who you don't say, "How are you?" to – you know they'll tell you at length!

There were a lot of notable long-standing Chellaston residents. People would come in regularly and have a sit down on one of our chairs – one would come in every week and we'd get her a taxi and she'd sit down while she waited. I was satisfied by the fact that people valued the community pharmacy; people speak highly of the service we provided. The effort you put in was appreciated.

Healing power of prayer

I obviously think it is (important) and many people do. Various studies and surveys show that if people think someone's praying for them, they do get better quicker. Whether that's the positive thinking of the person themselves, when they know someone else is concerned about them and praying for them, who knows? It's not one of those quantifiable things. I've known situations where people have got better unexpectedly when others have been praying for them. Whether that is the power of prayer or whether it would have happened anyway, you can't say. Why it happens, who knows, but that's what faith is – it's believing something that you are unable to scientifically demonstrate.

In studies done with hundreds of people split into those people prayed for and those who weren't, there was a statistically significant difference in recovery rates of those that were prayed for. Admittedly it was done by a Christian organisation, and that may have inherent bias; it wasn't a randomised, double-blind trial, more a survey.

Call to the Ministry

David left the pharmacy in 2008. He spent 5 years training for the priesthood. He became curate at St Michael and St Mary's, Melbourne. He is now vicar of St. John the Evangelist, Hazelwood, Derbys.

I haven't always been a church-goer. I would guess I've always been a believer, but I wasn't confirmed until the year I got married, 1991. I didn't go to church up until then - up until my middle twenties. Once I started going to church, I started becoming more involved in the church: being on the Church Council, leading prayers - St. Werburgh's in Spondon. The minister there was the minister who used to be here at Chellaston, Richard Andrews.

I trained at first to be a lay reader, a licensed preacher and teacher. Even before I finished that reader training, I felt that I was being called to being a priest. You go through a selection process: I spoke to various vocations offices and other ministers and Richard is a kind of mentor and they affirmed for me that they thought this was the path for me to follow. I initially thought I would be a non-stipendiary minister – a non-paid minister – in secular employment in the pharmacy. But when I went for my selection meetings they said, "No, you ought to think about doing it full time", so I spent some time talking with my family, some time in prayer and then thought, "Yes, let's do that; give up pharmacy and be a priest and do it full time".

The family have been supportive the whole way along: we're a church family – my wife's been going longer than I have. She was fully supportive of me being ordained to be a priest; she was less expecting I would be giving up my job as a pharmacist; that was a surprise to both of us. God moves in mysterious ways, we don't know why. You follow a calling – I never heard God speaking to me but there was a strong feeling that this was the right thing to do.

I enjoy church services on a Sunday, I love weddings – such happy occasions - love doing baptisms. Funerals, you can't say you enjoy, but it's a good thing to do. You're able to help people; you're an important part of their lives – that's good. It's nice to be alongside people at those key moments, to make those moments easier for them, sharing people's journeys, struggles and experiences.